HOMESPUN

FAITH

The Rest of the Story
Volume One

By

Daisy Beiler Townsend

DEDICATION

To my beloved granddaughter, A. Joy Trumbull, who has certainly lived up to her name and brought much joy to our hearts by her wholehearted commitment to our Savior, Jesus Christ. I say with the Apostle John, *I have no greater joy than to hear that my [grandchildren] are walking in the truth (3 John, v. 4).*

ACKNOWLEDGEMENTS

I want to thank my husband, Donn, for his help, patience, prayers and support during the writing and publishing of this book. You have skills that I don't have, and I couldn't do it without you. I am so blessed to be your wife.

Also, many thanks to our friend, Doug Williams, who used his skills to make our cover much better than it was!

Also ongoing thanks to my faithful prayer partners who are always there for me when I feel the hot breath of the enemy on my neck: Angelyn Trumbull (my daughter), Bonnie Prugh, Cherri McAnallen, DeVonne White, MaryElla Young, and Stacey Pardoe.

INTRODUCTION

In 2014, a dream I'd carried in my heart for many years finally came true. I published Homespun Faith, Reflections on the Seasons of Life, the only book I ever intended to write. It was a book compiling the devotionals I'd written since 1977 with many more devotionals I wrote to fill in the gaps. It became the story of our lives thus far in devotional form.

Beginning in 2016, I started another journey, joining many authors who share their thoughts with others through a weekly blog. It gave me a great deal of joy to share my life with some of my readers, passing along nuggets of Homespun Faith as God continued to teach me and mold me into His image.

Even before I finished my historical Christian series, Sarah's Legacy, Sarah's Legacy Shared, Sarah's Legacy Tested, and Sarah's Legacy Lived, I knew I wanted to share the material from my Homespun Faith Blog in a wider arena by publishing it in Homespun Faith, The Rest of the Story. I have chosen to identify the devotionals not only by a title but by the date it was written.

 A great deal has happened in the eitght years since I published the first volume of Homespun Faith. I actually think I've done some of my best writing as we walked through fiery trials, and I hope this book will be a blessing to you. Perhaps God will use it to prepare you for whatever He has in store for you.

As I said at the end of the Introduction to the first volume of Homespun Faith, we hope that you will enjoy the journey and that these devotionals will inspire you to look for God in the everyday happenings of your life so that you, too, may acquire "homespun faith!"

LEARNING TO BE CONTENT
March 21

All my life I've gleaned nuggets from Scripture, devotionals, and various other sources that have woven "Homespun Faith" into the fabric of my soul. My desire is to share some of those nuggets with you–fresh manna that will help to nurture and feed your spirit and grow your faith.

Today I want to talk about learning to be content. Sarah Young says she wastes so much time and energy yearning for different circumstances. For example, longing for warmer weather if it's cold, cooler weather when it's hot. And I believe complaining about the weather is the great American past time!

I am *so* guilty of this! When our daughter, Angelyn, was small, one of her favorite sayings was, "If only I had (that book, that bike, that ?), I would be SO happy!" But regardless of whether or not that item was received, it wasn't long until it was something else that would be necessary to make her "SO happy!" (Thankfully, I think she's long since passed that stage!)

While I'm not so apt to think that some item would make me happy, I do have a tendency to think if only God would solve "this problem" (whatever it may be–usually relational since nothing affects me more than a broken relationship), I would be SO happy! But soon there's something else it will take to make me happy. If I'm temporarily too busy, I long for less to do, and if I'm bored, I long to be busier.

I'll never forget my mother's prayers when it became necessary for her to move to Goodwill Home near the end of her life. Almost every time we prayed together, she would say, "Oh Lord, help me to be content whatsoever state I'm in." She didn't want to grumble and complain, losing her joy and making those around her unhappy as well. Of course, Mother was praying Scripture, as she often did, quoting the Apostle Paul in Philippians 4:11b, "for I have learned in whatever state I am, to be content" (RSV). (NIV says "for I have learned to be content whatever the circumstances.") Wow! I want that!

However, I'm encouraged that even the Apostle Paul said this was something he ***learned***–it did not come naturally. If he could learn to be content even in prison cells with conditions worse than we can imagine, perhaps there is hope for those of us who live in much better conditions to LEARN to be content.

Holy Spirit, work in our hearts an attitude of gratitude regardless of the circumstances. Let us take seriously Paul's words, *If anything is excellent and praiseworthy--think about such things"* (Philippians 4:8 NIV).

GODLINESS WITH CONTENTMENT
March 28

A male cardinal repeatedly crashed into our living room window years ago when we lived in Sandy Lake. Sometimes he fell to the ground, stunned, only to get up and try again. One day I said, "Silly bird! Don't you know you'd be miserable in our house?"

Soon after, a friend told me, scornfully, about the first house she and her husband owned, (a small ranch style with an orange and brown kitchen), and her longing for a nicer house. Remembering the cardinal, I looked around at their lovely spacious home with every modern convenience and wondered if she was happy.

About a year later she sat in our living room and wailed, "I hate my life!" Eventually, she left her husband and children and moved into a small apartment. The large, beautiful house had not brought happiness. Although she was a Christian, she hadn't learned that "only Jesus can satisfy your soul."

I was sobered by my friend's experience and reminded of the day I'd made a decision to be content. I'd always loved our Sandy Lake home and never thought of being dissatisfied until we began attending a new church. Many of our new friends had more affluent lifestyles than we did, and I began to feel self-conscious about our house. It was well over a hundred years old and a bit shabby—especially the carpet which we couldn't replace because of my allergies. Would our new friends look down on us when they discovered where we lived?

One day while weeding our flower bed, I spotted discontentment growing in my heart and saw it for what it was: a nasty weed, a temptation from the enemy of my soul. I realized I could entertain this "weed," allowing it to grow and choke out my joy, or I could pull it up. I chose contentment with the home God and my hardworking husband had provided, recognizing that true friends would love me regardless of where I lived. I pulled the weed.

In Exodus 16 when the children of Israel complained to Moses, he said, "Your complaints aren't against us, they are against God." We often fail to recognize when we complain that our complaints are really against God and His provision for us. Complaining was one of Israelite's greatest downfalls in their wilderness journey, and it can be ours as well. Few things make life more miserable than a complaining spirit.

Recently, we had the opportunity to visit my sister, Ruth, in the lovely home she shares with her husband, Harold. I love visiting them, enjoying their hospitality and their beautiful home. As I sat on the couch looking at my surroundings, I felt only joy at God's provision for my sister. I rejoiced that it's possible to delight in what God has provided for someone else, while being completely satisfied with what He's given me. The Apostle Paul was right when he said, *Godliness with contentment is great gain* (I Timothy 6:6 NIV).

Father, help us to be quick to spot the weed of discontentment in our hearts and to pull it before it pollutes our souls. Amen.

(Author's note: I've learned cardinals are territorial and this cardinal was likely fighting a perceived intruder (his reflection), but at the time, he appeared to be trying relentlessly to get into our living room.)

FOR PERFECT, WE HAVE TO WAIT FOR HEAVEN
March 21

A few years ago Donn and our grandson, Connor, built a birdhouse. It was a great little house, and we were excited when a pair of wrens came to build a nest. But almost immediately an English sparrow showed up to bully the wrens. He would stick his head into the hole and even try to enter while Mama and Papa wren were home, or go right in when they weren't. I was furious at this invasion, and soon Donn made a smaller hole in a board, just the right size to fit over the first entryway, and nailed it in place.

I have to admit I took great delight in watching that bully try his best to get into our little blue birdhouse, poking his head repeatedly, and fruitlessly, into the hole. He continues to do this every year during nesting season, and I'm still ecstatic each time he fails.

At first I wanted to focus on what lesson I could learn from the foolish behavior of the sparrow—and there are many. But instead, I found myself thinking about my reaction to his failure. Why do I feel triumphant and happy, even gleeful, every time he tries to shove his head through that tiny opening? Could it be that most of us desperately want to see bullies brought to justice, or at least fail resoundingly? And that we hate it when they seem to get away with brutish behavior and make innocent "wrens" suffer?

I think we feel like the psalmist who said, *But as for me, my feet had almost slipped; I had nearly lost my foothold*, (Psalm 73:2 NIV) when he saw the prosperity of the wicked. He talks about the carefree lives these "bullies" appeared to lead in comparison to his own, implying he'd gained nothing by keeping his heart pure and doing what's right. He can't make sense of it. Ever feel that way? I have.

But God didn't leave the psalm writer there. In verse 17 Asaph says, *When I tried to understand all this, it troubled me deeply **till I entered the sanctuary of God; then I understood their final destiny.** (NIV* emphasis added) Ah, there you have it. When we **enter the sanctuary of God**, when we allow Him to show us an eternal perspective, we remember that our lives here are fleeting. Living with eternity in view reminds us it isn't the outcomes here but the *final destiny* that really matters. At last, with eternity in view, the psalmist recognizes it's the wicked, the bullies, who are on "slippery ground" (Psalm 73:18).

Does that mean we don't fight the bullies (English sparrows) when it's in our power to do it? That we just stand passively by waiting for them to receive their "final destiny?" Not on your life. Jesus said, "Whatever you did for one of the least of these brothers of mine, you did for me" (Matthew 25:40) NIV, and "Speak up for those who cannot speak for themselves;" (Proverbs 31:8 NIV). So we do all we can, but we do it with eternity in view and the knowledge that this life is not all there is.

We were created for Eden and all of us, in one way or another, yearn for perfection—a perfect world, perfect justice, perfect outcomes. But if we want to be content as the Apostle Paul says he learned to be, we have to accept that we will never get perfection here. Because for perfect, we have to wait for heaven.

Father, show us how to fight the "bullies" in our lives without losing the contentment that comes from maintaining a heavenly perspective.
Amen.

TESTED BY PROMISE
October 25

What comes to mind when you remember the Israelite's deliverance from Egypt? I admit I usually think of their repeated doubt and unbelief. I had completely forgotten their initial reaction to God's promise of deliverance in Exodus 4:29-31 NIV.

*Moses and Aaron brought together all the elders of the Israelites and Aaron told them everything the LORD had said to Moses. He also performed the signs before the people, **and they believed.** And when they heard that the Lord was concerned about them and had seen their misery, they bowed down and worshiped.*

So in the beginning, the Israelites believed! Georgia Burton in The Upper Room says, *How excited the Israelites must have been, knowing that God would deliver them! Perhaps they imagined a quick, easy exodus. Instead, their predicament got worse. Pharaoh wasn't about to release them simply because Moses told him to; in fact, he imposed tougher demands on them. So rather than bowing down and worshiping God, they complained.*

Do you remember the story? In Exodus 5 we find that after Moses and Aaron told Pharaoh about God's request that he let them go to worship God in the wilderness, Pharaoh stopped providing the Israelites with straw to make their bricks. They were required to make the same number of bricks, but they would also have to find their own straw. When the Israelites didn't make their quotas, Pharaoh's overseers beat them. The Israelites were angry with Moses and Aaron and in turn, Moses was angry with God!

In spite of God's promise to deliver them, the Israelite's deliverance was not going to be quick and easy and often ours isn't either. Receiving what God has promised may require that we go on believing even when it looks like He has failed us and like He isn't keeping His Word.

Many times in the Bible, circumstances got worse before God's promises became reality: Joseph was imprisoned before becoming a leader; Abraham was asked to sacrifice his son before becoming the father of nations; Paul was blinded before becoming an apostle to the Gentiles... (Georgia Burton)

Sometimes we have to go through things to prepare us to receive what God has promised. I get the impression Joseph was a proud young man when God gave him the promise in a dream of others bowing down to him, but after going through a devastating series of events, he was ready to fulfill the huge task God gave him. Abraham had to be willing to sacrifice his beloved son so Isaac wouldn't become an idol to him. Proud, self-sufficient Paul had to be blinded and led by the hand to begin the process of becoming whom God had promised Ananias he would be, *God's chosen instrument to proclaim my name to the Gentiles and their kings and to the people of Israel. (Acts 9:15 NIV)*

So if God has made and confirmed a promise to you, don't be surprised if things happen that make you doubt His Word, if things get worse instead of better. I Peter 1:6-7 NIV says, *In all this you greatly rejoice, though now for a little while you may have had to suffer grief in all kinds of trials. These have come so that the proven genuineness of your faith—of greater worth than gold, which perishes even though refined by fire—may result in praise, glory and honor when Jesus Christ is revealed.*

Our faith is more precious than gold to God and we can expect it to be tested, even when it comes to receiving what He's promised.

Father, keep us steadfast in our faith in you even when things seem to get worse instead of better and your promises aren't fulfilled according to our timetable. Amen.

A TIME FOR HEAVEN
May 5

On Mother's Day many years ago, I looked out our kitchen window just in time to see a chipmunk eating baby cardinals in the nest outside the window. I screamed for Donn to bring his BB gun, but he was too late. I was furious even though I knew the chipmunk was just following God-given instincts.

A friend once accused me, "You're always for the underdog, aren't you?" One would think with that penchant, doing foster care would have been a natural direction for me. (Especially since I'd almost died giving birth to our twins, and we'd decided not to have more children.) However, I'd always resisted the idea of being a foster parent because I didn't think I could give up the children if the courts returned them to their biological home. Then one day, the Holy Spirit said, "What if God wants you to do foster care?" After that, it was only a matter of time.

When CYS asked us to take 18-year-old Sherry* and her two-year-old son as boarders, my bent to stand up for the underdog surfaced again. She had a boyfriend who often didn't show up for dates, yet told me with great emotion, "I *love* Sherry." One day I'd had enough. I glared at him and said, "Well you certainly have a *strange* way of showing it!"

Sherry watched wide-eyed as I gave George* a good-sized piece of my mind. Afterward she said, "I saw a side of you today I'd never seen before."

"I'm like a mother bear when someone messes with her cubs," I told her.

Another time when a mother had endangered her child, I said, "If you *ever* do anything like this again, I'll do everything in my power to see that you *never* have another opportunity."

James 1:19 tells us to be "quick to listen, slow to speak, and slow to get angry," but I believe there is a time and place for being angry, speaking emphatically, and taking action. Especially if we see someone

*(Name Changed)

being mistreated by a person or corporation bigger, stronger, and more powerful. Ecclesiastes 3 doesn't specifically address anger but it does say: "..a time to tear and a time to mend, a time to be silent and a time to speak, a time to love and a time to hate, a time for war and a time for peace..." (Ecclesiastes 3:7-8 NIV).

I'm told in Nazi Germany, people in a church near railroad tracks sang louder to drown out the screams of the Jews being taken to gas chambers at Auschwitz (concentration/extermination) Camp. Edward Burke said, "The only thing necessary for evil to triumph is for good men (*and women*) to do nothing."

I get Citizen Magazine, newsletters from American Family Assn., and emails from One Million Moms to keep me informed of rights being violated and evil prospering. Then I send emails, sign petitions, and make phone calls to stand for truth and righteousness in our nation and in our state. We can't take action if we are uninformed. Donn and I also pray about specific battles because Scripture tells us, "We wrestle not against flesh and blood, but against principalities, powers, and spiritual wickedness in high place" (Ephesians 6:12 KJV). And "The weapons of our warfare are not carnal but mighty through the power of God to the pulling down of strongholds" (II Corinthians 10:4 KJV).

If we believe as Christians we should always speak softly and agree with everyone, we have been deceived by the enemy of our souls. We serve a God whose Son drove moneychangers and animals out of the temple courtyards when they turned His Father's house into a den of thieves. Will we be as zealous to take action when we see God being dishonored or "the least of these" being mistreated? Or will we allow evil to triumph by doing nothing?

Forgive us, Father, when we bow down to the god of being nice instead of acting on righteous anger for the sake of your holy name and the least of these. Amen.

WE HAVE A CHOICE
May 20

Years ago I had a conversation with a woman from a Bible study in Penn Hills. I have no recollection of what the conversation was about, but suddenly *on the inside*, I was very angry. As far as I know, the woman never knew I was angry because I gave no indication. But *I* knew, and I couldn't get my inner reaction out of my mind.

Finally, I said, "Lord, what fruit of the Spirit am I lacking that I reacted that way?" I believe it was a Holy Spirit-inspired prayer because I'd never prayed that way before. There was no immediate answer, so I began to recite the fruit of the Spirit: Love, Joy, Peace, Patience, Gentleness, Goodness, Faith, and Self-Control. Hmmm... I knew there were nine fruit. Which one was missing?

When I looked at Galatians 5:22, I found my answer, Meekness. (Some translations have substituted the word "kindness" for "gentleness" and then used "gentleness" for "meekness," but I don't believe that captures the essence of this fruit as well.) I knew it was the fruit I lacked.

So I began to pray that the Holy Spirit would develop this fruit in my life. However, I found it's one thing to "appear" to be meek, but quite another to actually *be* meek. Webster says meekness is "enduring injury with patience and without resentment." Too often we endure injury, or what we perceive to be injury, by defending ourselves or by appearing to be meek while stuffing our true feelings. Neither is a healthy response.

Listen to the words of Jesus, "Come to me, all you who are weary and burdened, and I will give you rest. Take my yoke upon you and learn from me, for I am meek and lowly in heart, and you will find rest for your souls. For my yoke is easy and my burden is light" (Matthew 11:28-30 NIV). Jesus says, "Learn of Me, for I am *meek* and *lowly* in heart." What can we learn from Jesus about being meek and lowly in heart? (The picture was taken in Japan and is symbolic of life when we refuse the yoke of Jesus.)

It was impossible to affect Jesus by lowering His reputation for He had already made himself of no reputation (Philippians 2:7)...The man who does not think of himself more highly than he should (Romans 12:3) can never be hurt if others do not acknowledge him... a disease called "touchiness" is a morbid condition of the inward disposition. It is self-love inflamed to the acute point; conceit, with a hair-trigger...There are people who go about the world looking for slights, and they are miserable for they find them at every turn—especially imaginary ones." (Henry Drummond, Peace Be With You) So true!

Jesus' heart was free of pride, selfishness, and ambition which I believe are the opposite of meekness and lowliness of heart. For that reason, "When they hurled their insults at Him, He did not retaliate; when He suffered, He made no threats. Instead, He entrusted Himself to Him who judges justly" (I Peter 2:23 NIV). Our usual response to insults and threats is to defend ourselves, but we have a choice. We can choose to pray each day, "Enable me to bring my entire spirit, soul, and body under the reign of your Spirit. Teach me today to walk in the Spirit and not to fulfill the deep desires of my flesh."

Henry Drummond says, "We can (choose to) become meek and lowly in heart while the old nature is becoming numb from lack of use." I love that! We have a choice.

Lord Jesus, help us choose each day to come under the reign
of your Spirit rather than yielding to our old nature. Develop meekness in our hearts
as we choose to take your yoke and learn from you. Amen.

(Author's Note in 2020) As I've said in the past, there is godly anger, but I knew this wasn't it! I believe we've never lived in a time when we needed so desperately to remember we have a choice about how we respond to things that are said or done to us. We don't have to lash out and spew venom on anyone who disagrees with us and/or who lashes out and spews venom on us. We still have a choice in the year 2020!)

WHAT IF I GIVE ALL?
April 8

During our one-year term in Japan, Donn and I did a Bible study called "Loving Jesus." The author talked about the woman with the alabaster jar who showed lavish devotion to Jesus; then asked how we can express extravagant devotion to Him. "What did it cost the woman and what are the costs for you?"

God was already dealing with our hearts to come back to Japan for a longer time and these were heart-wrenching questions. What would it cost us? These were some of our answers: our family; our friends; our home; our cars; our church; our jobs; security. (Our family, friends, and church as in being distanced from them.)

Bruce Wilkinson had spoken at an OMS Conference before we went to Japan and said a little boy at the Conference asked him if he would make a donation to the OMS chiildren's mission project. Bruce said, "Tell you what, I'll give what you gave. How much did you give?" Without missing a beat, the little boy answered, "Oh, I gave all I had." Bruce said he took a deep breath and then emptied his wallet of its substantial amount of cash.

As we sang our theme song (What If I Give All?) at the end of almost every Japan presentation during the four years before our return to Japan, we thought of this little boy. What could God accomplish if we gave all we had? The end of the song says, "We cannot close our eyes and turn away, When we hear His Spirit call. We see the need, now let Him hear us say, "What if I give all? What if I give all?"

The process was every bit as heart wrenching as we anticipated, but I clung to scriptures like Philippians 3:7-8 NIV *But whatever were gains to me I now consider loss for the sake of Christ. What is more, I consider everything a loss because of the surpassing worth of knowing Christ Jesus my Lord, for whose sake I have lost all things. I consider them garbage, that I may gain Christ.* and Luke 12:33-34 *Sell your possessions and give to the poor. Provide purses for yourselves that will not wear out, a treasure in heaven that will never fail, where no thief comes near and no moth destroys. For where your treasure is, there your heart will be also.* These scriptures clarified our direction

When we sold our home and gave away or sold most of our furniture and many of our possessions in 2008, we didn't know if we would ever own another home. One of our granddaughters, then ten, said, "But Grandma, where will you live when you come back?"

"Oh, we'll have a house or an apartment somewhere, Honey," I responded. But we had no idea what the future held. Tokyo's cost of living is one of the highest in the world and our support needs were huge. We were committed to using every resource we had if the support we raised wasn't enough—Donn's retirement, the money we'd received thus far from the sale of our house (land contract), and my remaining inheritance after paying the cost of our first year in Japan. We didn't know if we'd have any resources left to begin life again in the United States after our service in Japan was done.

But God... In Matthew 6, He says, "Don't worry about what to eat, what to drink, or what to wear for your Heavenly Father knows you have need of them and He'll give them to you if you give Him first place in your life." (My paraphrase of verses 31-32.) Because of His amazing outpouring in various ways, we didn't have to use any of those resources, and we never lacked for anything. One of our supporters told us, "I don't pray for you that much, I just pray every day, 'Give them all the money they need, God!'" That prayer was abundantly answered.

When the Lord began to call us from Japan three years later, I started looking at houses online, mainly in Sandy Lake and Stoneboro where we'd lived before and in Grove City near our church. We never talked about it, but in the back of my mind I had a list of what I thought we needed in a retirement home: bedroom, bathroom, laundry

room on the main floor, and a garage, and on my wish list, a family room. Homes that met my criteria in our price range were almost nonexistent.

The night we discovered we weren't going to New Zealand (a real possibility—but that's a story for another day), I couldn't sleep and searched again for houses online. I discovered there were three pages of houses for sale in Greenville—I'd only skimmed one page the few times I'd even looked in Greenville. There on page three was a house that met every criteria I had for about half the price we'd thought we'd have to pay. But Greenville? I never wanted to live in Greenville. However, two of our children and three of our grandchildren lived there, so maybe it wouldn't be so bad...

I left the website open, praying that if this was God's provision for us, Donn would be excited and would want to pursue it. He was and he did... We arrived in the States on August 4 and on August 5, we signed an agreement on this house and settled on August 31, 2011. Donn's mother passed away shortly before we returned home and his sister put Mom's furniture in storage until we were ready to use it. We miss her terribly but love using her things with precious memories. We also love this indication of God's provision for us.

Later we learned that God had "gone to prepare a place for us" here in Greenville fifty years earlier. At that time, the owner had added a "mother-in-law's wing" which accounted for the bedroom, bathroom, laundry room, family room (her living room) on the first floor of an older, two-story home—almost unheard of in this area! (We also discovered that just a few weeks before we returned, the seller had dropped the price $30,000!) In addition, it soon became clear that almost everything God had for us to do was in Greenville!

This is the second time God has asked us to give all we had, and in both cases as we were obedient to Him, He has gone to prepare a place for us that was beyond anything we could ask or think (Eph. 3:20). He is a faithful, amazing God.

Father, help us trust you
enough to surrender all we have to you. Enable us to believe
you are faithful. Amen.

FAULTY GPS
May 30

How do you feel about your GPS? Most days I love it until something happens to remind me it isn't infallible. Like the day Donn and I decided to ask "Sam" (short for Samantha) to direct us to Walmart on a cross-country trip. As we wound our way deeper and deeper into the boondocks, my trust level dipped to an all-time low. Finally, Sam chirped, "Arriving at Walmart, on your right." There was absolutely nothing on our right, and certainly not a Walmart! Spurning Sam's help, we relied on Donn's sense of direction to get us back to civilization.

Then there was the day we went antiquing in Myrtle Beach, depending solely on Sam to find the shops. Repeatedly, she took us to places that gave no indication of ever having been antique shops. The last straw came when she guided us directly to the locked gates of a gated community! It was a disappointing end to our hopes of spending a leisurely afternoon enjoying antiques.

These experiences paled, however, when compared to a newspaper headline I read in a devotional recently, "Man Follows GPS Directions and Drives Car into River." Wow! We've had some bad experiences with our GPS but nothing this drastic. The author of the devotional said the driver of the car was on an unfamiliar road, traveling at night in the fog. "He believed the GPS directions were correct, unaware that the unfamiliar road ahead ended in disaster." (The Upper Room)

As important as it is to have good directions to find a given destination when we travel, how much more important it is to have trustworthy instructions to discovering God's will for our lives. Following wrong or incomplete guidance can end in disaster. Years ago I read about a woman whose dog loved to lie at her feet. But every time she stood up, the dog dashed to the bottom of the stairs, assuming that's where she was going. One day she told him, "If you want to be with me, you'll have to learn to follow me."

She cringed as she heard what she'd said. "Lord, please don't tell me I'm like this foolish dog!" But as she thought of the many times she'd waited to hear only part of what God was saying before she "dashed to the bottom of the stairs," she knew He was right. Proverbs 19:21 says, "There are many devices (schemes) in a man's heart, but the counsel of the Lord, that shall stand" (KJV).

I don't know about you, but it doesn't take me long to come up with a *good* idea. But if we're serious about following Jesus, we have to discover whether the "good ideas" we have are just that, or whether they're "God ideas." II Corinthians 5:15 NIV says, *And (Jesus) died for all, that those who live should no longer live for themselves, but for Him who died for them and was raised again.*

The same day I read about the "Misguided GPS," I also read the following from another devotional: *Discovering God's will is an ongoing adventure with rewards along the way. His Word is our map for the journey, and the Holy Spirit is our guide, who provides 'road signs' as we travel.* (In Touch) Much more dependable than a GPS!

How are things going in your life journey? Did following a "Misguided GPS" leave you in the "boondocks" or in front of a locked gate? If you've been living your life for yourself rather than for the One who died for you, it's not too late to change. Jesus is waiting for you to "make of your body a living sacrifice," (Romans 12:1-2) so that He can live His life through you. You can begin the exciting adventure of discovering His plan for your life with His Word for your map and the Holy Spirit for your guide.

Heavenly Father, forgive us when we forget that we are not our own, that we are bought with a price. Help us glorify you in our bodies (I Corinthians 6:19-20 NIV). Amen.

THEOLOGY 101: I'M NOT GOD
June 6

The morning our granddaughter, Joy, graduated, a song that seemed totally inappropriate for this "joy"ful occasion kept intruding on my thoughts...

'Cause what if your blessings come through rain drops
What if Your healing comes through tears
What if a thousand sleepless nights are what it takes to know You're near
What if trials of this life are Your mercies in disguise.
(Blessings by Laura Story)

I couldn't understand why God would put this song in my heart on Joy's graduation day... until I heard the "Challenge" brought to the seniors by their Bible teacher, Pastor Jeremy. He talked about what a tough year it had been for these six seniors. He told us how their faith had been tested and tried, dealing with unanswered prayers and unexplained situations. He took us to Job 38 where God asks Job some difficult questions after his horrendous losses:

Where were you when I laid the earth's foundation?
Who marked off its dimensions?
Who stretched a measuring line across it?
On what were its footings set, or who laid its cornerstone--
(Job 38:4-6 NIV)

Pastor Jeremy talked about taking these students to "Theology 101." Then he asked one of them, "Which is?" The answer was prompt, "I'm not God." Wow! Theology 101 is I'm Not God! No, I'm not. I don't have the advantage of seeing things from God's perspective. I don't know the reason behind the things that happen. Job never knew why he was bombarded with devastating trials. If he had known, it wouldn't have really been a test.

"Nobody would ever call Job 'blessed' after all his losses," Pastor Jeremy told us, "but James 1:12 says, 'Blessed is the man who perseveres under trial...'" The Amplified Bible says, "Blessed (happy, to be envied) is the man who is patient under trial..." That is so foreign to our culture. Truly, God's Kingdom is the World's Kingdom upside down. Our idea of blessing may be totally different than God's idea.

> *We pray for blessings, we pray for peace*
> *Comfort for family, protection while we sleep*
> *We pray for healing, for prosperity*
> *We pray for Your mighty hand to ease our suffering*
> *And all the while, You hear each spoken need*
> *Yet love us way too much to give us lesser things*
> (Blessings by Laura Story)

At Joy's graduation, we were reminded that we often overlook the fact that it was God not Satan who initiated Job's testing. *"The Lord said to Satan, 'Have you considered my servant Job?'"* God knew what Satan's response would be. The first time I realized this, I said, "God, you set him up!" As we wrestle with this truth and wonder why, it takes us back to Theology 101, "I'm Not God!" We don't have the advantage of seeing things from God's perspective. However, another Laura Story song gives us some clues.

> *You give and take away for my good*
> *For who am I to say what I need?*
> *For You alone see the hidden parts of me*
> *That need to be stripped away.*
> (Bless the Lord by Laura Story)

Recently I was commiserating with a young couple whose eight-year-old daughter has diabetes. Responding to my sympathy, this wise young wife said, "God produced things in our character through the suffering that accompanied our daughter's diabetes that were not there before." Sounds a lot like Romans 5:3-4, "...*We know that suffering produces perseverance; perseverance, character; and character hope...*"

Years ago while traveling, Donn and I visited a church that might have had trouble with this theology. We were singing *Blessed Be Your Name* along with the worship team when we realized they'd changed Matt Redman's bridge from "He gives and takes away" to "Whatever comes my way." They might also have trouble with the Psalmist who said, "It was good for me to be afflicted that I might learn your decrees" (Psalm 119:71 NIV).

So as it turned out, the song the Lord put in my heart on Joy's graduation day was totally appropriate. I give thanks for the godly pastor who walked with our granddaughter's graduating class this past year. The things God taught them through him are bedrock foundation not only for seniors but for all of us.

Father, thank you for loving us enough to teach us lessons we don't even know we need to learn. Help us to trust you as you develop in us the bedrock faith of Theology 101. Amen.

(Author's Covid 19 Note – It seems appropriate to revisit this devotional at a time when, around the world, we need to enter Theology 101, I'm Not God! None of us have the wisdom to understand all that the world is going through, but we can ask God: "What lessons do you want to teach us through the trials and tribulations of the year 2020?" I'm praying that when this year is over, we will not have gone through these experiences in vain, but will have grown and matured as we learned the lessons God had for us.)

BLESSINGS IN DISGUISE
June 12

I quoted a song in a previous devotional by Laura Story that contains the phrase, *What if trials of this life are your mercies in disguise?* Several days later in my Upper Room devotional, the author told of praying that a suspicious mole on her arm would disappear without medical intervention. Her prayer wasn't answered, so she went to a dermatologist.

To her surprise, the doctor wanted to biopsy another spot on her skin—one that hadn't concerned her at all. When the results came back, the second site, rather than the first, had been diagnosed as early-stage melanoma, a deadly form of skin cancer. If God had answered her prayer for the first mole to go away, the other spot would have gone undiscovered. Her unanswered prayer was a blessing in disguise.

Over the last week or so, I kept hearing the phrase, "blessing in disguise." The staff at the Comfort Inn where our Beiler Reunion was held forgot to set up the Conference Room for us. Donn and I swept, scrubbed tables and set up the room ourselves which resulted in them giving us a $40 discount. Donn suggested that perhaps it had been a "blessing in disguise" that Wendy had forgotten to set up the room.

All of this prompted me to think about other times when God had given me or others "blessings in disguise." The biggest was when our twins were born while Donn was in graduate school. At my eight-month visit when the Dr. suggested there might be two babies, I said, "We  can't have twins. We live in an efficiency apartment!" Donn was undaunted by the news, but I was appalled at the terrible timing of this event.

As it turned out, Donn's semester break came right after our twins' birth so he could help 24/7 to feed babies, wash diapers, make formula, and carry laundry up and down the stairs. Even after he went back to school, he came home between classes to help with all these responsibilities for the first seven months. (By God's grace, he did all this and still graduated from Purdue with a 5.82 GPA. Purdue used a 6.0 GPA equivalent to most schools 4.0 GPA)

Even so, it wasn't until Donn went to work eight months later and I began caring for Angie and Robbie alone in our three-bedroom house that I recognized the timing of their birth as a "blessing in disguise." How wise our Heavenly Father had been to give us our twins while their earthly father's schedule allowed him to help with all the tasks that would have overwhelmed me alone. I realized it had also been a "blessing in disguise" to have only a small apartment to keep clean during those early months.

Sometimes, blessings in disguise are even more difficult to recognize than ours. Years ago I heard a speaker tell about the death of her son. She said he was on fire for the Lord and had a bright future ahead of service for Him when he was killed in a car accident. As she stood beside his casket, she told the Lord, "No good will *ever* come from this!" The words were barely out of her mouth when her prodigal daughter came to her and said, "Mom, I want to come back to the Lord so I'll see Steven again some day."

In retrospect, I realize that our inability to recognize "blessings in disguise" are often "Theology 101:I'm Not God" occasions. We don't have the advantage of seeing things from God's perspective, only from our own. We may recognize the blessing later, but during those in between times: "We need to evaluate our circumstances in light of God's character, not evaluate God's character in light of our circumstances" (Bruce Wilkinson).

Father, help us not to malign your name when
our circumstances seem anything but blessings in disguise.
Enable us to trust that you work all things together for good to those
that love you and are called according to your purpose (Romans 8:28
NIV). Amen.

HE'LL CALL AGAIN
June 23

When the Lord began speaking to Donn and me about Japan, we thought we'd go to OMS Japan in August, 2001, on a ten-day mission trip and then decide if it was a good fit for us. However, first we went to the OMS annual Conference in July where OMS was celebrating 100 years of ministry. Bruce Wilkinson (Prayer of Jabez) was their keynote speaker with the theme: "Expanding Your Borders."

After his first message on Friday morning, Bruce told us OMS had a goal at this Conference of having at least 101 people volunteer to go into OMS missions for six months or more. (We had been given a hand out when we came in that day with places to check showing the length of time to which we were willing to commit. Bruce gave us an opportunity to go forward if we were ready to make that commitment.) I was ready, but when I looked at Donn in a "What's your answer?" manner, he said, "Maybe, but I'm not ready to sign on the dotted line yet." Bruce had said he'd give another opportunity the next day, so for the rest of that day I waited and prayed.

Before we went to bed that night, Donn told me, "I think we can go and shake Bruce's hand tomorrow." He went on to tell me how God had spoken to him and put his mind at rest about this decision. When Bruce gave the invitation on Saturday, we almost ran to the front along with many other volunteers. I believe the total for the two days was 110 people. It was an amazing experience.

The next day we started our eight-hour trip home, planning to stop at a church along the way to worship. Watching the time and looking for churches that started at the appropriate time, we pulled into the parking lot of the First Missionary Church. The name seemed to fit the occasion and that day, their Director of Missions was speaking. Rev. Mann spoke passionately about the urgent needs in missions.

He told about a little boy named Billy who lived down the street and was hanging out with him as he put an addition on his house. Billy's mother called him once for lunch, then twice, then the third time. Rev. Mann said, "Billy, your mother's calling you. This is the third time she's called. Don't you think you should answer?"

Billy responded, "No, it's okay. She'll call again."

Our speaker said, "I believe that's often how we respond when God calls us. We just ignore Him and say, 'It's okay. He'll call again.' " Donn leaned over and whispered, "If I hadn't said 'Yes,' I'd be feeling so convicted right now!"

We believe the Holy Spirit led us to that church as another confirmation to our call to missions. Of course, God knew that Donn was going to respond to the second call the day before, but I was comforted by the fact that even if he hadn't, God already had another opportunity planned for him at the First Missionary Church the following day!

The Bible is filled with accounts of people God called who didn't say yes the first time, Jonah being perhaps the most famous. After going in the opposite direction and surviving a deadly experience, we're told in Jonah 3:2, "Then the word of the Lord came to Jonah a second time." This time he went!

Then there was Moses who responded to God's call with a series of questions and excuses, ending with, "Pardon your servant, Lord. Please send someone else." He went only when God promised to send Aaron to do the talking. (Exodus 4:13)

Gideon also questioned God's choice of him (the least in his family), and God's choice of someone in his clan, "My clan is the weakest in Manasseh..." (Judges 6:15). He asked not for one sign but for two. There was also Barak who declined to do what God commanded him unless Deborah went with him. (Judges 4)

I certainly don't advocate ever ignoring God when He calls, but in the end, it isn't our first response that counts but whether or not we ultimately obey. In Jesus' parable of the two sons, the first son responded to his father's request to work in the vineyard saying, "I will not," but later went, while the second son said, "I will, sir," but did not go. Jesus said, "Which of the two did what his father wanted?" (Matthew 21:28-31) Obviously, it was the first son in spite of his initial negative response.

So where do you fall in the spectrum of willing to unwilling when God calls? I have never been so tempted to ignore Him, or pretend I didn't hear, as when He first began to speak to me about Japan, but what rich experiences and relationships we would have missed if I had. And God only knows what "Jonah-type" storms we may have encountered. If you think the cost of obedience is too high, ponder instead what the cost of disobedience may be.

Father, forgive us when the cost of obedience seems too high and we choose to ignore you. Help us trust that Psalm 18:30 NIV is true: "As for God, His way is perfect." Amen.

I KNOW WHOM I HAVE BELIEVED
June 29

In February of 1983, my father was diagnosed with a malignant brain tumor. He came through surgery well but radiation therapy took its toll, leaving him weak and frail. Around Thanksgiving of that year, I took him and my mother for a doctor appointment where we learned that the tumor had returned. The doctor said he had six weeks to live.

Receiving this kind of diagnosis often tends to bring out differences of opinion and belief among Christian families. Some people were saying, "You need to have faith that he'll be healed." Others said, "You need to accept that he's going to die." Everyone seemed to know what the right thing was to believe, everyone except me.

Filled with turmoil and confusion, I took a walk and cried out to God, "What do *I* believe?" Immediately a still small voice whispered, "I know *Whom* I have believed and am persuaded that He is able to keep that which I've committed unto Him against that day" (II Timothy 1:12 KJV).

Peace permeated my heart as I meditated on that verse. I might not know *what* I believed about whether my father would live or die, but I knew the One in *Whom* I believed, the One who knew His plan for my father, the One I could trust with the final outcome. And I was persuaded that I could safely commit my father into His keeping.

Since Daddy was saying he wanted to trust God to heal him, I took my cue from him. Before we went home, I told Mom, "As long as healing is what Daddy wants, I'll pray with him for healing. If he changes his mind, I'll follow his lead." I returned to Sandy Lake at peace about trusting God with my father's health.

A few weeks later, he went into a coma and when he regained consciousness, he told Mom, "I don't want to fight anymore. I just want to go to be with Jesus." I sensed Daddy's home going would be soon and prepared to return to Maryland. On our way, I told the Lord, "I'm not quite ready to let him go. Could you give me a little more time?"

The week that followed was one of the most precious in my life as it related to my relationship with my father, which had sometimes been difficult. What a blessing to finally be able to do things for him—he'd never really needed my help, always having been strong and healthy. I told him it was a blessing, not a burden to take care of him. I read Scripture to him and discovered we had a mutual love for the 12th chapter of Romans. I laughed at his jokes, delighted that he never lost his sense of humor.

What a great gift God gave me, peace to surrender my father to Him and grace to enjoy one more memorable week. When someone dear to him complained that it wasn't fair that her father, who wasn't serving the Lord, was in good health while my father, who loved Jesus, was dying. Daddy said softly, "But I'm ready to go, and he's not." Daddy died on Christmas day at age 67, going into the presence of his Savior.

If you find yourself in a situation where you don't know *what* to believe or *how* to pray for a loved one, commit them into the hands of the One in *Whom* you have believed, being persuaded that He is able to keep them and bring about His purposes for their lives.

Father, when we struggle so hard to believe the *right* things in difficult situations, enable us to surrender control and place our loved ones in the keeping of the One in whom we have believed. Amen.

JACK STORIES
July 6

This is one of my favorite anecdotes taken from an article by Geneen Roth called Big Fat Lies. She says, "My mother has a name for the elaborate, wrongheaded tales we tell ourselves. She calls them Jack Stories."

"One day, Jack had a flat tire on the side of the road--before cell phones, AAA, GPS, etc. He saw a farmhouse in the distance and started toward it to ask if he could use the phone. As he got closer to the place, he told himself this story: There will be a man at home, and he will be mean, nasty, and maybe even violent. He will answer the door and ask me what the heck I think I'm doing, out in the middle of nowhere, knocking on a stranger's door. He will assume I am a thief or a louse. He probably won't care that I have a flat tire. He won't care about his fellow man. He is probably the kind of guy who kills small animals just for fun. He might even try to beat me up.

"Just as he is approaching the front Door, Jack thinks: *This guy is an absolute menace to society. I would be doing everyone a favor to take him out.* Jack raps on the door. Hard. Loud. A man answers and Jack says,, "So! There you are! You swine, you pig! Well, take this—!' And Jack punches him in the nose."

I laugh every time I think of the poor, clueless guy who answered the door only to be punched in the nose for no reason. But I also wonder how many hapless folks I've "punched in the nose" because of Jack Stories I've told myself.

Our former pastor, Dick LaFountain, had another name for Jack Stories, he called them, "Stinkin' Thinkin'! "Mindreading," one of the ten negative thought patterns of stinkin' thinkin,' is defined this way: "You assume to know what others are thinking. You perceive yourself as being able to read their thoughts, intents, meanings, and motives—and it is always negative. Rarely do you ever read positive thoughts into people's expressions or actions..." That definition sums up Jack pretty well, except that Jack had never even met the man in the farmhouse!

Sometimes we make up Jack Stories because of experiences we've had as children. As a little Mennonite girl getting on a public school bus with our Amish neighbors, we got lots of rejection. As a result, in other situations, I often assumed, for no good reason, that people would reject me. My Jack Story might have gone something like this: "I know these people won't like me. They probably think I'm stupid and won't want anything to do with me. I'd better avoid them." Rather than punching people in the nose, I kept my distance, in essence, rejecting them before they had a chance to reject me, although I didn't see it that way.

Other times, we tell ourselves Jack Stories out of fear. "If I perform in the talent show, I'm sure to make a fool of myself. I'll probably forget the words or sing the wrong notes. Everyone will think I'm an idiot." Or because of stereotypes we've believed. "White people are not to be trusted. Two of them took advantage of my sister and I've hated white people ever since. I'd have to be a real nut case to think they really want to be my friends."

It's true that some temperaments have a tendency toward more negative thinking than others, especially melancholies. However, Tim LaHaye did a study on the fruit of the Spirit with a football team and discovered that for every temperament weakness, there is a fruit of the Spirit which will compensate for that weakness if we allow the Lord to develop it in us. So there's never an excuse for saying, "This is just the way I am" when it comes to negative thinking.

In my experience, Jack Stories that do the most damage happen when I assume I know what someone is thinking or why someone is doing something (their motives), and respond based on those assumptions. If I want to know why someone did something, it's best to ask them, rather than assuming that I know. Ecclesiastes 7:8-9 NIV says, *...patience is better than pride. Do not be quickly provoked in your spirit for anger resides in the lap of fools.* and James 1:19 NIV *My dear brothers and sisters, take note of this: Everyone should be quick to listen, slow to speak and slow to get angry.* If we follow these instructions, we will be less apt to do foolish things as a result of Jack

Stories we've told ourselves.

Pastor Dick says these ten negative thought patterns are ten lies of Satan and I agree. (Sometimes Satan encourages us to tell ourselves these Jack stories and other times, he tells them and we agree!) "These thought disorders of the mind cause anger, bitterness, and depression," Pastor Dick concludes. So I challenge you, next time you find yourself angry, bitter, or depressed, check to see if you or the enemy have been telling you Jack Stories!

Father, show us the Jack Stories we've believed and reveal the truth to us. Help us remember that "Love always believes the best" (I Corinthians 13:7 Amplified). Amen.

HOW TO RESPOND TO REJECTION
July 15

A seasoned writer said, "When you have enough rejection letters to paper your wall, then you are a real writer." That being the case, I certainly qualify as a "real writer!" If I had saved all my rejection slips, I could paper many walls. Although many of my articles, devotionals, and stories were published in magazines and periodicals, they were far outnumbered by the rejections.

Each time a rejection slip arrived, I had a choice. I could give up or I could persevere. Sometimes persevering meant recognizing that I needed more training. I took a college course in Rhetoric and Composition, as well as in Creative Writing. I also took a yearlong course in fiction writing through the Writer's Digest School of Writing and attended writer's conferences and workshops.

But first I had to determine that my desire to write was strong enough to overcome all the negatives that go along with writing. The following excerpt of the devotional, *Stewards of God's Gifts,* from my book, Homespun Faith, tells of my struggle.

"I want to write, Lord. I really want to write."

I don't know how many times I said those words as I fretted about the lack of time in my schedule for writing, but today a clear response penetrated my ongoing litany.

"Do you, Daisy? Do you really want to write?"

The words hung in the air, confronting me, challenging me. Did I really want to write? Was I serious enough about writing to put up with the aspects of it that I didn't enjoy, or was it something I liked complaining about without having any intention of taking serious action?

It was a painful process, but eventually I had an answer. I wanted to write. I was tired of whining and ready to take action. There were still hurdles to overcome, but those things were actually of secondary importance now that I'd settled the major question..."

Many others much more famous than I were also faced with the choice of whether or not to give up when they failed. Before inventing a commercially viable electric light bulb, Thomas Edison is said to have failed over 10,000 times. When asked by a newspaper reporter if he felt like a failure and if he should give up after having gone through over 9,000 failed attempts, Edison simply stated "Why would I feel like a failure? And why would I ever give up? I now know definitely over 9,000 ways an electric light bulb will not work. Success is almost in my grasp." Wow! That's perseverance!

Henry Ford of the Ford Motor Company, one of the most successful automotive companies of all time, had two failures that ended in bankruptcy before he succeeded with the present Ford Motor Company. Walt Disney was fired from Kansas City Star because his editor felt he "lacked imagination and had no good ideas," and Amy Grant's own mother told her, "I don't think singing is your gift, Amy." One of the most renowned presidents of the United States, Abraham Lincoln, had a monumental list of failures before becoming the 16th president of the United States.

In her devotional, Running the Race, in the Upper Room, Judith Wege says, "The idea is that a 'real' writer doesn't quit but perseveres. A real writer keeps running the race." I believe that's true whatever our profession or vocation. Hebrews 12:1 says, "… let us run with patient endurance *and* steady *and* active persistence the appointed course of the race that is set before us." (AMP)

We're called to be stewards of the talents and abilities God has given us, no matter how many times we fail. How we use those gifts may change in different seasons of our lives but the Holy Spirit will direct us to the "good works, which God prepared in advance for us to do" (Ephesians 2:10 NIV) if we don't get discouraged and give up.

Father, forgive us when we refuse to develop the gifts you have entrusted to us. Help us remember we are only stewards, not owners, of the abilities you have given. Amen.

WITHOUT WARNING
July 27

Donn and I spent a lot of time in the Lazy River at an indoor water park a few years ago. Eventually it occurred to me that our experience with this Lazy River ride was a lot like life. One minute we were floating along, relaxing without a care in the world, and enjoying the experience. The next minute we were battling to avoid going through the tunnel where we would be drenched, and then trying valiantly to get past the spot where we were repeatedly becalmed.

In a similar way, seldom do we have any warning in life that we're about to encounter a battle that will rock us to the core and make our carefree life a distant memory. Last week we received a prayer request for the husband of one of the young women who was in my Apples of Gold group ten years ago. He's been diagnosed with an aggressive stage 4 inoperable brain tumor. They have three children. Until a few days earlier, there was no indication that he wasn't completely healthy.

Many of us have been told medical tests revealed cancer in us or one of our loved ones or that someone we love has died or been injured in an accident. Sometimes the crisis involves discovering that a husband or wife has been unfaithful to us or to a loved one. Regardless of the source of the bad news, there is seldom any warning, and we often find ourselves unprepared for the deluge of fear and emotion that accompanies the news.

Psalm 107 was one of my mother's favorite chapters of the Bible. Possibly because she was the go-to person for many in our community when they found themselves in desperate situations. This chapter tells us that no matter what kind of trouble people found themselves in, whether of their own doing or through no fault of their own, when they "cried out to the Lord in their trouble, He delivered them from their distress." This scenario is repeated four times in verses 4-9, 10-16, 17-22, and 23-32. Sometimes it was necessary for God to mete out discipline before they were willing to cry out to Him.

My mother's favorite verses in this chapter were verses 29-30.

"He stilled the storm to a whisper; the waves of the sea were hushed. They were glad when it grew calm, and he guided them to their desired haven." When I read these verses, she would invariably take a deep breath and let it out in a long, "Ah....!" That was the desire of her heart for those who came to her for prayer.

Another part of our Lazy River experience that seemed to parallel life was the patient lifeguard who came to our rescue again and again. He watched for us and repeatedly threw out a "lifeline" that we could grab to help us regain momentum and get through the rough spot. He never acted annoyed or impatient no matter how many times He'd rescued us before. I realized how like the Lord he was in that respect. When we need to be rescued many times, we often become embarrassed to ask for help—again! However, our Heavenly Father is infinitely patient when we are flailing about ineffectually. Psalm 103:14 says He remembers that we are dust.

As I think of our patient lifeguard at the water park, I realize that each time we struggled, we always had a choice whether or not to accept his help. We could have chosen to go on struggling alone. The same is true in life. I wonder how often we fight on alone when God is stretching out a "rescue device" to bring us to a desired haven. The choice of whether or not to accept His help is always ours.

Father, forgive us when we choose self-reliance,
self-sufficiency, and independence instead of crying out in our distress
so that you can rescue us. Help us learn to cry out to you
as our first option. Amen.

DO YOU NEED HELP?
August 3

I ended a previous devotional with a prayer asking forgiveness for our self-reliance, self-sufficiency, and independence. Those words stirred up memories of the events God orchestrated 16 years ago to expose the deep roots of those issues in my life.

It all began innocently enough with a conference I wanted to attend in North Carolina. I decided to travel by bus to keep my travel costs low since driving that far alone would deplete my energy levels—a fibromyalgia issue. I made sure the motel recommended was within walking distance of the church where the conference would be held. I didn't know anyone else who planned to go to the conference so I would travel alone. No problem. I could do this.

The bus trip was a bit more complicated than I'd anticipated. Diesel fumes made me nauseous and what I thought were scheduled stops to pick up more passengers were actually transfers to different buses. Each time we stopped, I had to collect my luggage, carry it into the bus station as well as into the bathroom if necessary, then lug it back to the new bus. But, I could do this!

At last we reached my final destination. I took a taxi to my motel from the bus station and got settled. Now to get directions to the conference location. When I explained where I was going, the desk clerk told me there was no way I could walk. There were no sidewalks and it was a busy highway. So I took a taxi to the first session of the conference and was alarmed at the cost. Then I discovered because of the long breaks between sessions, I would need to go back to my motel between sessions or be stuck at the church all day every day with no place to rest. Dollar signs were flashing before my eyes.

Someone suggested I have the conference moderator ask if anyone else was staying at my motel with whom I could travel. I was unprepared for how difficult it was for me to make that simple request, and I considered renting a car instead. I felt like such a loser for being in this dilemma.

At last I approached the moderator, and at the end of the session, she explained my situation to the group. My feeling of being a loser increased. As the session ended, all the insecurities and fear of rejection I'd experienced during my Mennonite childhood flooded back. I sat alone, on the verge of tears, unable to believe my inner turmoil. What if no one wanted to help me? What if no one offered? In my eyes, it would be public rejection.

I could barely speak when a tall, lovely woman approached and asked if I was the one who needed a ride. She said she was alone at the conference and would be happy to provide transportation. She was driving a luxury car, and again I felt like such a failure. This woman had it all together.

However, soon I found myself telling my rescuer why I was hardly able to talk when we met. I told her about my reaction to finding myself needing a ride and how hard it had been to be the one needing help.

My new friend, Jennie,* was quiet, and I didn't know what she was thinking. We were constant companions during the conference, going out to eat and sitting together at sessions. As the Holy Spirit began to show me the deep roots of my self-reliance, self-sufficiency and independence and His desire to free me, I shared with her what He was showing me. She told me surface things but nothing personal.

One day at lunch, Jennie finally broke her silence and began to share at a deep level. She and her husband had just separated and she had come to the conference, wanting to hear from God. The car she was driving was a rental because her old car wasn't safe to travel that far. The car rental company had upgraded her to the luxury car, no extra charge, because they didn't have any economy cars left.

I believe I was the first person she'd told about the separation because trust didn't come easily to her. She said if I hadn't needed a ride, she would probably have stayed aloof from others throughout the entire conference, but when the moderator shared my situation, the Holy Spirit prompted her that He'd provided this car for her to share. Now I was in tears again. I had been *so* upset about needing to ask for help, but God in His goodness, had already provided a luxury car for transporting me to

*Name has been changed.

and from the motel.

As Jennie shared more details about her life, I listened, counseled and comforted. We became good friends and stayed in touch for many years. She and her husband reconciled and the last I knew, they were still together. The Holy Spirit had a task for me at the conference that I'd have missed if I'd pursued my self-reliant, self-sufficient, independent way.

After I got home, my lessons in learning to accept help continued. One day in a Walmart aisle, I looked up at the shampoo I wanted, well out of reach, and then glanced at the people around me. I spotted a tall teenager nearby, but I couldn't bring myself to ask for help. Having noticed my predicament, he smiled at me and said, "Do you need help?" Although I'd been unable to make the request, I was able to answer a firm "yes!"

When I finished getting my groceries and drove home, I carried in one load of groceries leaving the car door and our screen door open. The phone rang. Caller ID told me it was a call I needed to take. A few minutes later, my dear friend and neighbor, Jan, breezed into the house, a bag of groceries in each arm. "No, no," I told her, "you don't need to do that!"

With a smile, on her way back out for more groceries, she answered, "But I *want* to do it!" I wondered how often I'd denied people the pleasure of doing things for me because of the tendencies I've mentioned..

I've since realized that those tendencies are highly valued in the United States of America, but not so in God's Kingdom. First and foremost, He wants us to depend on Him, His strength, His grace, not on ourselves. Secondly, He has called us to be interdependent, not codependent, on others in the Body of Christ. When we portray ourselves as not needing anyone or anything, we rob others of the joy of being involved in our lives. The first step to overcoming these tendencies is recognizing that we have them. The Holy Spirit will help us if we ask.

Holy Spirit, reveal any tendencies we have to self-reliance,
self-sufficiency, and independence. Help us rely on you, depend on you,
and make you our sufficiency, Jesus, as well
as being interdependent with others. Amen.

Do Something
August 12

Donn and I went to a Pittsburgh Pirate's baseball game last Saturday night. We arrived early and discovered the Saturday Night Block Party on Federal Street. It included live music which I love, so we stood near the bandstand enjoying the music, wondering why we hadn't done this before.

In front of the bandstand, there was a large open area for dancing, although few were using it. Then I noticed an older woman in gray shorts and T-shirt dancing, getting closer and closer to a man who, as far as I could tell, she didn't know. Soon she began pressing parts of her body purposefully against him. He responded by smiling and pointing to the area of contact as she began to rub her body against his. Their gyrations became more and more lewd and obscene as another man joined them. Wide-eyed children stood on the sidelines and other people snickered and laughed.

I looked around for someone who would put a stop to this, but there was no one. A still small voice reminded me that *I* was someone. Gathering my courage, I walked across the open area. I addressed the man first, reminding him that there were children present. He nodded and walked to the sidelines. When I spoke to the woman, she wouldn't meet my eyes or acknowledge my presence, but she too moved to the sidelines until I walked back to where I'd been standing.

When the woman initiated and the behavior began again, we went to look for someone in authority and I began to pray silently, taking authority over lust. We walked quite a distance before we found an employee of the Pirate organization. He pointed out a police officer nearby. When I told the officer what was happening, he asked for a description of what the people were wearing and headed for the bandstand. We followed. By the time we got back, the woman had disappeared. After a few minutes, I told the officer she was gone and thanked him for checking.

On the way home, I couldn't get the disgusting images out of my mind---images that children had also seen---and my anger grew. Donn and I discussed what had happened and I told him about God reminding me that *I* was someone. Then in the background on K-LOVE I heard Matt West singing…

If not us, then who
If not me and you
Right now, it's time for us to do something
If not now, then when
Will we see an end
To all this pain
It's not enough to do nothing
It's time for us to do something.

On Monday I called the Pittsburgh Pirate Organization to complain that no one in authority was at the Block Party to stop the lewd behavior. Chris, who is in charge of the Block Parties said she would discuss it with her staff and make arrangements for one of them to be near the bandstand in the future.

But then she said that although she agreed with me that this kind of behavior shouldn't happen, it would be hard to judge someone for what they were doing because they weren't naked! I reminded her that it is possible to be lewd and obscene without being naked, and said, "If there is no law in the city of Pittsburgh to stop that kind of behavior, there should be."

Then I asked Chris, "If people who believe in decency, as you say you do, and will not take a stand with those who don't, what will be the result?

All this reminded me of a man named Phineas in Numbers 25. He knew that he was "someone" and did something about behavior that dishonored God. An unnamed Israelite was flaunting his behavior in a public arena just as the woman and men were flaunting theirs on Saturday night. Phineas, the grandson of Aaron the priest, didn't stand around wondering why someone didn't do something. He put a stop to it. I'm not suggesting we employ he method he used (putting a spear through both of them) but that we follow his example of doing something. Listen to what God said to Moses about Phineas:

"Phineas...has turned my anger away from the Israelites. Since he was as zealous for my honor among them as I am..."

Wow! God said Phineas was as zealous for God's honor as God was! Would He say that about you and me? Are we zealous for God's honor? How do we respond when people around us do or say things that dishonor Him? Do we laugh at behavior or jokes that dishonor God or condone it by our silence?

I wonder how many Christians were at that Block Party, snickering and laughing at the lascivious behavior or condoning it by their silence. God is looking for those who are willing to be like Phineas who was as zealous for God's honor as He is. He is looking for Christians who will "Do Something" about the things that dishonor God in our culture. Will you be one of them?

Father, forgive us for the times we have not been zealous for your honor because we are more concerned about offending others, forgive us for caring more about what others think than we do about your honor.
Forgive us for not doing something. Amen.

TRANSITIONS
August 17

Recently I was asked to speak to a group of interns about transitions. I agreed because I've had plenty of transitions! God knew from the beginning that I didn't have a bone in my body that could do the same thing for my whole life, so He's blessed me with many different seasons (Ecclesiastes 3:1). Each time a season changed, it required a transition.

In fact, one of the early truths God taught me was that there would be many seasons in my life in which I would use different gifts and abilities. He didn't want or expect me to use every ability in every season. The harder truth to grasp was that *He* would decide when it was time for a season to change. I could create a lot of problems for myself and others if I refused to let go when a season was over.

For example, before our children went to school, I sewed many

of our clothes* because, as a stay-at-home Mom, that season required that I spend a lot of time at home. But after our children were in school, God gave me other responsibilities.

Instead of enjoying the new season, I wrestled with guilt because I wasn't making clothes—especially when my mother said things like, "It's a shame someone who can sew like you do isn't using that talent." Years later, my mentor told me, "If you're going to be controlled by the expectations of other people, you can't be controlled by the Holy Spirit." We have to choose who we want to please: God or people.

(*In these pictures, we're all wearing clothes I made during that season.)

Here's what Romans 12:1-2 says: *I beseech you therefore brethren by the mercies of God that you make of your bodies a living sacrifice, holy and acceptable to God, which is your reasonable service.*

Be not conformed to this world but be transformed by the renewing of your mind that you may know *what is that good, perfect and acceptable will of God* My definition of making of our bodies a living sacrifice is allowing *God* to decide what we're going to be or do or where we're going to go in these bodies during each specific season. Only when we follow these instructions can we *know* what we're doing is the *good, perfect and acceptable will of God.*

However, there are some things I love to do so much that it's been hard to let go when it was time for a season to change. The first time God called us out of foster parenting in 1998 and there were no children in our home for the first time in 25 years, I thought this change of seasons would be the death of me. (I still dream often that Donn and I are in various situations taking care of children.) Even though foster parenting is hard, I missed not only the children, but all the other people who were in my life because of our involvement in foster care.

So I started training to be involved in CASA which would allow me to be involved in the lives of foster children without them living in our home, even though God had called me to a counseling season. It was my way of trying to hang on to the previous season. I soon discovered that God doesn't give grace to go on doing the things from a previous season. He only gives grace for the current one. If we try to hold on, burn out or ineffectiveness is sure to follow. I had to give up my plan of being a CASA worker during my counseling season.

It can be tricky to discern between our emotions and the leading of the Holy Spirit during transitions. Proverbs 19:1 says, *There are many devices (plans or schemes) in a person's heart; but the counsel of the Lord, that shall stand* (NIV). Just because we LOVE doing something or can do it well, doesn't necessarily mean it's God's plan for us in this season. That excited, *woo hoo* feeling we get at the thought of doing something we love may just be our flesh getting all excited, not the direction of the Holy Spirit.

Years ago I read about a mental picture God used to teach an author a lesson about this issue. She saw herself entering a banquet hall where people were doing many interesting and exciting tasks. So she approached the head waiter, asking what job he had for her. He directed her to a table with one leg shorter than the others where 14 people were seated. He said her job was to hold up that corner of the table so the people seated there could eat without the table rocking.

The woman was disappointed, feeling that she was qualified to do something much more important and exciting, but as she began to concentrate on the job she'd been given, watching the faces of the people who were seated at her table and seeing how much more pleasant their meal had become as their table stabilized, she forgot about all the other jobs she'd wanted to do.

As the author thought about this mental picture, she realized their were fourteen people to whom she was giving support, and the head waiter, Jesus, would not be impressed if He found her doing a job she considered more important or interesting than the job He'd given her. When she cried out to Him, as most of us do, "But Lord, what about what other people expect of me?" He answered her, "What I expect is more important." We must not allow our flesh to draw us or people to guilt us into taking on or staying in roles that do not fit our present time and season.

Father, forgive us when we care more about pleasing others than pleasing you. Help us make of our bodies a living sacrifice, being willing to allow you to guide and direct our lives. Amen.

.

LET UP ON THE THROTTLE
September 8

Some of you know that on Monday, August 22, I ended up in the Emergency Room with a 4.9 mm kidney stone which they sent me home to pass. I also ended up with a kidney infection because my left kidney was blocked by the stone and the CRNP forgot to give me a prescription for an antibiotic.

Two miserable days later, my doctor hustled me into the hospital to insert a stent to drain the kidneys, kept me overnight to give me antibiotics intravenously, then sent me home to recover. The fun was just beginning! The stent puts pressure on the kidney/bladder which has kept me close to home ever since.

What you don't know is that the previous week, I'd been feeling rather stressed. I'd even thought, "I feel like I need a rest." I was also having a lot of pain, a fibromyalgia flare—usually related to stress. On Saturday morning when I bent over to pick up my purse, my lower back went into spasms (another stress symptom), and I couldn't stand up. In a partially bent-over position, I backed up and managed to flop down on our bed.

I walked slowly and slightly stooped for the rest of the day and didn't attend our grandson's football scrimmage or church on Sunday. Sitting on a bleacher, a Sunday School class chair or a church pew didn't sound like good options. When I asked the Lord what this was all about, I felt prompted to look at our calendar.

I realized that four out of the previous six weekends, we'd been gone at least part if not all of the weekend—Sundays especially being the day when I try to rest. Although I'm taking a break from counseling to finish my book, I've been pushing hard on that. When it comes to writing, I'm my own boss, and Donn has commented more than once that my boss is a slave driver! I began to understand why I felt like I needed a rest.

I've had lots of time to evaluate all this over the past couple weeks of my enforced rest, and I heard in my spirit, "Let up on the throttle." It was the title of a Daily Bread devotional I remembered from years ago. The author* talked about WW I planes that were not equipped with throttles for slowing down or speeding up. He said constant full speed ahead took its toll on the engines. When throttles were added, these instructions came with them: "Takeoff power (full power) may be used for only a maximum of five minutes." Bob Griffin in his book, *Cleared For Takeoff* said, "The pilot was instructed to back off from full power as soon as possible. Trouble was ahead for those who ignored the warning."

Are you getting the picture? The author says, "God did not create us to run at full speed all the time. We may race for a while with open throttle through our Christian lives, packing our time with one activity after another, but if we don't slow down occasionally we are headed for burnout or a crash landing." He's so right.

Although there have been unpleasant, painful aspects of the "rest" God has provided, my blood pressure is down, my TMJ symptoms are gone, and I feel so rested and relaxed. Those less desirable aspects of my rest have give me a renewed commitment to make a practice of "Letting up on the throttle," to live life at a slower pace."

*Only the author's initials, DCE, are listed on the Daily Bread devotional I saved.

How about you? Are you running at full speed ahead? Do you need to let up on the throttle?

Jesus said, Come to me, all you who are weary and burdened and I will give you rest. Take my yoke upon you and learn from me, for I am gentle and humble of heart, and you will find rest for your souls. For my yoke is easy and my burden is light (Matthew 11:28-30 NIV).

Father, show us how to rest and relax in ways that will keep us from burning out or having a crash landing. Help us tune in to what our spirits, souls, and bodies are saying to us about their need for rest.
Amen.

ORDERED STEPS
September 18

I've been thinking lately about our steps being ordered by the Lord (Psalm 37:23). I believe this is true on any given day when we're yielding to the Holy Spirit and trusting Him to guide us. However, on some days it becomes more evident than others that He's guiding our steps. Remembering them makes me smile or sometimes takes my breath away!

Years ago I was driving through Amish country every few weeks on my way to the chiropractor just across the Ohio line. The sign "Brown Eggs" outside an Amish farm house drew me and I stopped there to buy fresh eggs several times. One day, on a whim, I told the Amish housewife, "I thought you might be interested to know that my parents were raised Old Order Amish."

She beamed. "Where was that?"

"I was raised in Grantsville, Maryland."

Her dark eyes sparkled, "My mother was adopted by an Old Order Amish family from an orphanage in Grantsville, Maryland!"

I was amazed. "Who adopted her?" The name meant nothing to me but she told me the family was from Oakland, Maryland, a town about 28 miles from Grantsville.

"If you'll send me a letter telling me when you'll be down this way again, I'll make sure Mamm is here to talk to you."

I did as she asked and a few weeks later, I met her mother. When I told her my mother was Ruth Beachy, daughter of Mose Beachy, she gave me a huge smile. "Why yes, I knew Ruth! The family who adopted me lived on a farm next to her uncle in Oakland. We played together when they came to visit her uncle."

This dear lady knew my mother's childhood nickname, as well as the nicknames of her younger brother and sister. It was so exciting to talk to someone who had known my mother in her childhood. We reminisced for some time about those days of long ago.

This incident gave me a warm sense of my steps being ordered by the Lord simply because of the joy He knew it would bring me and my new friend to have this encounter. It's a memory I cherish. There are other times, however, when it's obvious God has a greater purpose for ordering our steps.

One day I stopped in to visit our former next-door-neighbor in Penn Hills where we'd lived for three years. Donna answered the door, crying, phone in hand. After she hung up, she told me she'd just learned that Karen, the woman who'd bought our house, was going to take them to court to force them to remove the part of their paved driveway that was on her property.

I felt responsible because, although we'd given our neighbors permission to pave the part of their driveway that was on our property, we'd never put anything in writing. We'd known when we bought the house that part of the neighbor's gravel driveway was on our property and part of our fence in the backyard was on theirs. It was true of most of the houses in the neighborhood. No one cared. Until now.

Heartbroken that the person to whom we'd sold our house was causing trouble for our former neighbors, I prayed with Donna on the spot, and Donn and I continued to pray for a peaceful resolution after I returned to Sandy Lake. I can't remember how long we waited or even who told us the outcome, but Karen never took our neighbors to court. Soon after her threat, one of the neighborhood children got hurt on the gym set in her back yard—a broken arm or wrist, I think. Karen was so afraid she would be sued by the parents of the child who'd been hurt that suing someone else was the last thing on her mind.

What were the chances of me arriving at Donna's door just as she'd received the news that they were going to be sued? I believe God ordered my steps that day so that we could intervene through prayer. He cared about what was happening in our old neighborhood and gave us an opportunity to join Him in bringing about a different outcome.

I love the idea of my steps being ordered by God and often when I find myself in unusual places (like the emergency room or a traffic jam), I'm learning to ask Him "Is there any particular reason why you needed me here?" More often than not, there's someone or some situation for which He wants me to pray.

Thank you, Father, for ordering our steps,
sometimes to bring us joy and sometimes so we can bring joy to
someone else. Help us stay tuned in to the voice of your Spirit so we
don't miss out on the blessing. Amen.

COMPELLED BY LOVE
October 10

About a week ago, I sat on our front porch basking in the peace of our lovely neighborhood in Greenville. I couldn't help remembering all the years I'd spent disliking this town! When we lived twenty minutes away in Sandy Lake, I came here as little as possible—for groceries, doctor appointments, sporting events and birthday parties (two of our children and now four of our grandchildren live here). I had decided Greenville was a depressing, dying town.

We'd always thought when we returned from Japan, we'd live in Sandy Lake where we'd lived before or in Grove City where we went to church. However, we hadn't found a house suitable for our retirement years in our price range in either of those places. Then I discovered one in Greenville with everything we needed at a ridiculously low price.

I clearly remember that moment of decision where I almost bypassed this house because I disliked the town. But I surrendered my will and God made His plan clear.

A few short weeks later as we drove into Greenville on the way to meet our realtor, I noticed a sign on a business I didn't remember. "Fresh Grounds, Caffeine for the Soul." I told Donn, "I bet that's Marty's place!"

I'd known Marty Johnson for years, being good friends with his mom, Barb Johnson, and had run into him at a Hempfield School Open House before we left for Japan in 2008. He had told me about the donation they'd been given to buy a business in Greenville and the vision the Holy Spirit had given them of a coffee house that was also a ministry.

I was pretty sure we were looking at the culmination of that vision. Excitement bubbled up in me. I couldn't wait to get inside. I'm still in awe of what God did between the day I heard the vision and the day we saw it with our own eyes. I felt sure this was one of the reasons we were in Greenville. Being part of the Tuesday morning Downtown Ministries' prayer group became been one of my greatest blessings.

Now, five years later, I can hardly believe how much I've come to love this town. We prayer walk here and I weep for neighborhoods struggling with poverty and drugs. I know it's our mission field.

Several months ago, I talked to a missionary whose theme when she spoke at our church was, "The love of Christ compels us..." (II Cor. 5:14). When I talked to her about the years we'd served in Japan, she wondered whether the compelling love of Christ would allow us to stay in Greenville. I realized later that her thinking overlooked the fact that the compelling love of Christ isn't necessarily given to us only for a foreign land.

Some months before we'd started prayer walking, I had taken a break from going to Fresh Grounds for prayer meeting when my counseling schedule got busy. Then Donn and I began to feel led to prayer walk in a part of Greenville that concerned us. The first day we walked, I wept and cried and told Donn, "I have to go back to Fresh Grounds; it's where we pray for this town." The love of Christ compels me to pray for Greenvillle, for the ministries here, and for opportunities to be the hands and feet of Jesus.

The love of Christ still compels us to pray for the people of Japan. (We will return to minister there with One Mission Society from October 28 to November 7, 2016.) But just as surely, the love of Christ compels us to pray for the people of Greenville and to minister in the town in which we now live.

Seek the peace and prosperity of the city to which I have carried you into exile. Pray to the Lord for it, because if it prospers, you too will prosper (Jeremiah 29:7 NIV).

ALL ABOUT GRACE
November 10

On September 19, 2016, when my last stent was removed from my kidney, I assumed I'd take it a little easy for a week and then do spring housecleaning. That didn't happen! I had underestimated how long it would take me to recover from a kidney stone/kidney infection, two procedures in less than a month, and a month of physical inactivity. Most days I was so exhausted by noon that I had to lie down for several hours or take a nap before I felt up to doing anything.

As the days passed, I became concerned because we had scheduled our first trip back to Japan for the end of October. We planned to return to OMS Japan in Tokyo, the mission organization we'd worked with before, for ten days. From past experience, I knew the trip to Japan was a killer even when I was in tiptop condition. What would it be like in my weakened state?

I wanted God to endow me with super energy now so I'd be sure I could handle the trip and the busy schedule we'd have. Instead, I sensed He was asking me to trust that His grace would be sufficient for me regardless of how unprepared I felt physically. So I did what I could, continuing to make plans for our time in Japan, taking care of myself and packing.

Besides these concerns, I was also concerned about Donn because he hadn't handled the flights to and from Japan well for quite some time, withdrawing emotionally and barely eating the entire long trip. When we came home from Japan in 2011, I didn't know if he'd ever be willing to go again. But my yearning to reconnect with our former students had become so strong that I had told him if he didn't want to go, I would go alone. He'd decided to go, but I didn't know how he'd respond to the long flight. Would it have the same affect on him as it had before? But again I sensed the Lord wanted me to trust Him.

As it turned out, from start to finish, this trip was all about God's amazing grace. On the twelve-hour flight to and from Japan, I never experienced the exhaustion that I had before and Donn was his normal cheerful self for both trips. Extended layovers in Detroit on our way home were usually my worst nightmare because of my extreme weariness, but this time, when I had every reason to feel that way, I didn't.

I didn't lie down to rest at all in Japan because it's imperative for me to stay awake to get my body adjusted to the fourteen-hour time difference between PA and Japan, but in spite of that, the only day I was tired was our last Sunday there following an extremely busy week. Since we were only going to be there eight days, there were many people to see in that short time.

God's providential hand was so evident that I couldn't doubt that this trip had been His plan. Here are a few examples.

1) Before we went to Japan, one of the missionaries had  contacted me to ask if I would do chapel time for one of my former English classes. As I looked through Homespun Faith, my devotional book, praying about what to share, I saw the devotional I'd written about our friend, Yuko, whom we had led to the Lord in 2002. It occurred to me that since Yuko would be with us at this English Class, it might be a powerful thing to share her story of how we'd met and how she'd come to Christ as our chapel time.

I emailed to get her permission, which she gladly gave. I shared her story and afterward during lunch, the pastor's wife asked her many questions about her testimony in Japanese so the beginner's in the class were also able to understand. It was an awesome time. Many seeds planted for the Kingdom.

2) On our first Sunday, we had lunch at the cafeteria with the Seminary Church, and a young woman I'd met in 2009 sought me out to ask if I remembered her. She had an eating disorder and I remembered her well because her name had been on my prayer list ever since. Her eating disorder is better but I was able to pray with her about other issues. She doesn't get to church there often, so it was providential that she "happened" to be there the same Sunday we were.

3) We held an Open House for our former Seminary students who'd attended our English classes, and I learned that the husband of one of my former students has an aggressive form of cancer. He had just come home from a lengthy hospital stay—they are missionaries and live

on the TBS Campus near where our Open House was held. I went with a group of students, now pastors or pastor's wives, who gathered round him at his house and laid hands on him to pray. It was truly God's timing that allowed him to be home from the hospital at just the right time.

4) Another ministry we'd had in Japan was an Alpha course, which later grew into an English Bible Study. We had a potluck open house for our former students and one woman came who had completely dropped out of involvement in any OMS Japan ministries. She told me she had become a hikikomori (a person who doesn't leave their house) and wasn't involved in anything.

Later, R said she thought my coming to Japan was God's way of giving her a hint that He wants her to become like she was before, not isolating herself from everyone. She added, "I want to buy your book and maybe it will change my life."

I am still in awe of the energy and stamina that God gave me throughout this trip from start to finish. It was good for me to know that unless He came through, I wouldn't be able to accomplish what He'd sent us to do. So while at times, He reminds us to "let up on the throttle," at other times, He asks us to lean on Him for the endurance and strength to do what we could otherwise never accomplish!

Father, thank you for the reminder that nothing is too difficult for you. May we truly believe, as the Apostle Paul did, that "when I am weak, then He is strong." Amen.

THANKSGIVING DAY DEBUNKED
November 23

While most of us associate Thanksgiving Day with a table laden with turkey, stuffing, mashed potatoes, and pumpkin pie, it's meaning goes much deeper than that for Americans. (Sometimes I even forget that Thanksgiving Day is not an International holiday!) A Time Magazine website says:

Much is unknown about the first recorded feast between the Pilgrims and Native Americans in the New World at Plymouth in 1621, as historians have heavily relied on only two primary eyewitness accounts. But while a good meal is a constant, it's clear that the original festival doesn't have all that much in common with the all-American holiday recognized today, with its focus on football and, more recently, shopping.

So if the present all-American holiday doesn't capture the essence of that first Thanksgiving, what were the Pilgrims and Native Americans celebrating? Research shows that the Wampanoag Indians who attended the first Thanksgiving were key to the survival of the colonists during the first year the Pilgrims arrived and the celebration took place after the Pilgrims successfully harvested their first crops in autumn 1621

On at first Thanksgiving, I believe our ancestors were celebrating survival with those who helped them survive. Although forty five of the 102 immigrants who had come to Plymouth died during the first winter, thanks to the help of the Native Americans, the others survived.

Most of us have lives so far removed from the hardships of our forefathers that our mindset tends much more toward celebrating abundance than celebrating survival. Mere "survival" might be seen as failure on our part or even as an indication that God has let us down. Maybe we pride ourselves on "gutting it out" during tough times, but see no occasion for giving thanks. This is an attitude far from that of our ancestors or the prophet Habakkuk.

Though the fig tree does not bud and there are no grapes on the vines, though the olive crop fails and the fields produce no food, though there are no sheep in the pen and no cattle in the stalls, yet I will rejoice in the Lord, I will be joyful in God my Savior. (Habakkuk 3:17-18 NIV)

Wow! Compared to Habakkuk, I'm afraid I'm a failure at giving thanks in less- than-ideal circumstances. The Apostle Paul says, "Be joyful always, pray continually, give thanks in all circumstances; for this is God's will for you in Christ Jesus" (I Thessalonians 5:16-18).

In other words, give thanks even though we barely survived, even though life has been difficult, even though ________________. If we are believers in Jesus, we have His promise that He will never leave us or forsake us (Hebrews 13:5) and that He will work all things together for the good of those who love Him and are called according to His purpose (Romans 8:28). We still have reason to give thanks regardless of our circumstances.

Many years ago Donn and I wrote a song that came to mind this morning as I thought about this theme. This is the chorus.

Thank you for the flowers and thank you for the rain.
Thank you for the sunshine and thank you for the pain.
Thank you for the birds on wing and thank you for
the times we sing.
Thank you, Lord, we love you, Lord,
Thanks for everything.

Lord Jesus, enable us to give you thanks, in good times and in bad.

WHAT IF CLARK KENT FORGOT…
December 7

I've never been a big Superman fan. I guess I'm more than a little offended that the producers of the show think if Clark Kent takes off his glasses, I won't recognize him! However, recently I heard or read something about Clark Kent/Superman that I thought had great significance for Christians. Here it is:

What if Clark Kent forgot he was Superman?

What if he left his Superman cape hanging in the closet instead of putting it on before dressing as the meek, mild-mannered Clark Kent? He would have to respond to any crisis in his own strength, not with the powers of Superman. *What a waste*, we think. *He's Superman*! "Faster than a speeding bullet, more powerful than a locomotive, able to leap tall buildings in a single bound! This amazing stranger from the planet Krypton, the man of steel!" Yet he is being defeated every single day because he has forgotten who he is!

Does any of this sound familiar? What about us? We who are born again, spirit-filled sons and daughters of the most High God? Do we get up each day remembering who we are in Christ, or do we go about defeated every single day because we've forgotten?

Scripture tells us the same Spirit that raised Christ Jesus from the dead, lives in us (Romans 8:11). Jeremy Camp sings about this power:

The same power that rose Jesus from the grave
The same power that commands the dead to wake
Lives in us, lives in us
The same power that moves mountains when He speaks
The same power that can calm a raging sea
Lives in us, lives in us
He lives in us, lives in us

We are never told to be strong in our own power but to *be strong in the Lord and in His mighty power* (Ephesians 6:10). I John 4:4 says, *Greater is He that is in us than he that is in the Lord (* I John 4:4). Our hope is not in ourselves but in the Lord, *the Maker of heaven and earth* (Psalm 146:5-6).

We have hope
That His promises are true
In His strength
There is nothing we can't do
Yes, we know
There are greater things in store
We will not be overtaken
We will not be overcome
Greater is He that is living in me
He's conquered our enemy
No power of darkness
No weapon prevails
We stand here in victory
(Jeremy Camp)

If all these things are true, why are there so many defeated Christians? Could it be that we, like Clark Kent, have left our Superman cape hanging in the closet? Let's look at some specific instructions about the clothing we need to wear to be overcomers.

Therefore, as God's chosen people, holy and dearly loved, ***Clothe yourselves*** *with* **compassion, kindness**, **humility, gentleness and patience. [and forgiveness]**...

And over all these virtues **put on love** *which binds them altogether in perfect unity. (Colossians. 3:12-14)*

Therefore, **put on the full armor of God**, *so that when the day of evil comes, you may be able to stand your ground, and after you have done everything, to stand. Stand firm then, with the* **belt of truth buckled around your waist**, *with the* **breastplate of righteousness** *in place, and with your* **feet fitted with the readiness that comes from the gospel of peace**. *In addition to all this, take up the* **shield of faith**, *with which you can extinguish all the flaming arrows of the evil one. Take the* **helmet of salvation** *and the sword of the Spirit, which is the world of God. (Ephesians 6:13-17)*

So dear friends, while Clark Kent and Superman are only fictional characters who fight fictitious battles, the battles we fight are very real. If you identify all too well with Clark Kent who has forgotten who he is, I recommend two books by Neil T. Anderson *Victory Over*

63

the Darkness and *The Bondage Breaker* which will help you learn about who you are in Christ and how to use the Scriptures to be all that God created you to be. Don't give others reason to say, "What a waste. She/he is a Christian!"

Thank you, Father, for all the promises you've given us. Teach us everything we need to know so we can be *more than conquerors through Jesus Christ who loved us* (Romans 8:37). Amen.

THE POWER TO HURT US MOST
December 22

The other day I wrote in my journal, "It's always true that the ones we love most have the power to hurt us most." I was tempted, not for the first time, to stop "pouring myself out" for those I love.

Then I looked at the reference for my prayer promise for the day, John 3:16. I didn't even need to look that one up... "For God so loved the world that He gave..." I stopped. If anyone knows that the ones you love most have the power to hurt you most, it's God. He gave the ones He loved most (us) the very best He had (Jesus), and His heart was broken by our response.

John tells us, "(Jesus) came to His own and His own received Him not," (John 1:11) and Isaiah says, "He was despised and rejected--a man of sorrows, acquainted with deepest grief. We turned our backs on Him and looked the other way. He was despised, and we did not care" (Isaiah 53:3NLT). Jesus understands what it's like to be hurt by those for whom He has "poured Himself out," but He never stopped loving and never stopped giving.

But, you may say, how can I go on loving and giving to those who've broken my heart? There's only one key I've found to doing that... forgiveness. Every unforgiven act makes it more difficult to love the person who's committed that act. Forgiving doesn't come easily for me; and I do it only by the grace of Jesus who said as He hung on the cross, "Father, forgive them for they know not what they do." Many times when I think I cannot forgive offenses small in comparison to being hung on a cross, I've cried out, "Jesus, love through me and forgive through me because I can't do it on my own. Heal my broken heart and enable me to go on loving and giving."

The other day we were talking about forgiveness with our grandson who was reluctant to apologize. I said, "How do you think Papa and I have managed to stay married for 46 1/2 years? It's because we've gotten good at saying we're sorry and good at forgiving. We'd like to help you get good at it too." (Please don't take this as an encouragement to stay in abusive situations where you're being endangered physically and mentally by treatment from someone you love. Forgiveness does not constitute reconciliation in every case. There are times when we may need to separate ourselves from people, even while continuing to love and forgive.)

In this season of giving, forgiveness is the best gift you can offer those who've hurt you. Forgiving others is also the best gift you can give yourself. "Make every effort to live in peace with everyone...See to it that no one falls short of the grace of God and that no bitter root grows up to cause trouble and defile many." (Hebrews 12:14-15 NIV)

Refusing to forgive leads to bitterness which leads to all kinds of spiritual, emotional, and physical problems, defiling you and others. The Apostle Paul wrote, "If it is possible, as far as it depends on you, live at peace with everyone" (Romans 12:18 NIV). You can't do someone else's part but you can choose to do your own.

"It is hard to realize that the people we love are the ones who can hurt us the most—but forgiving is half the healing." (Unknown)

Holy Spirit, enable us to do what we cannot do in our own strength, continue to love and forgive. Amen

Darling of Heaven
January 5

A line from a song came to me this morning that always reduces me to tears: "The darling of heaven, crucified..."

Jesus, the darling of heaven. I had never thought of Him that way before hearing *Worthy is the Lamb* for the first time, never thought about how all of heaven must have mourned when their darling came to earth to be whipped, spit upon and crucified. For days that phrase kept

repeating in my mind... "the darling of heaven, crucified."

As a grandmother, I know our grandchildren are *my* darlings—no matter their age, no matter their size. (Strange as it may seem, my big, strapping twenty-five-year-old grandson is just as much my darling as when he was small.) I can't imagine watching them go through the treatment Jesus experienced.

One of my devotional readings today said, "Who do you love most fiercely, most protectively, most desperately here on earth?" (A Little God time) No secret what my answer would be. One of our grandsons told me recently how surprised he was at how mad I get at referees who aren't being fair to our team, and especially to our grandchildren.

Somehow thinking of Jesus as "the darling of heaven" sparks a deeper love and appreciation for the One who gave His life for me. I took some of our Japanese students to see The Passion of the Christ in Japan and was amazed to see standing-room-only crowds at the theater in the middle of a weekday. Those seated near me were weeping as they watched Jesus' brutal treatment. When I asked one of the students in my

Seminary English class what she thought of the movie, she said, "I want to preach the Gospel!" I wish we all had that reaction when we think about what "the darling of heaven" went through for us.

The rest of the devotional I quoted earlier went on to say, "Know that it is a mere fraction, nearly immeasurable, of what God would do for you. Spend some time thanking Him for His great love." What should our response be to the great love of our Father? Perhaps the hymn writer, Isaac Watts, said it best, *Love so amazing so divine, demands my soul, my love, my all* (When I Survey the Wondrous Cross).

Thank you for your great love for us, Father,
that sacrificed even the darling of heaven to make a way for us to be your sons and daughters. Enable us to respond to that great love with all our heart, soul, mind and strength. Amen.

DISCERNMENT AND GRACE
January 18

When Donn and I went to Japan for a year in 2003, one of my responsibilities was to teach the conversational English classes of a missionary who would be in the United States on home assignment. Soon after we arrived, I discovered that all eight of the conversational English classes were squeezed into a day and a half each week-- Wednesday morning and afternoon and Thursday morning.

I was stunned. I have fibromyalgia and one of the things I try to avoid is cramming too many responsibilities into a short period of time. When I overdo, a flare up of symptoms often follows. I thought the solution would be to move some of the classes to other days. However, our acting field director explained that our Japanese students often had many things scheduled, and if we changed the day, we would lose a lot of students.

Before going to Japan, the Lord had gone to great lengths to teach me that if I wanted to be guided by the Holy Spirit, I couldn't be ruled by the expectations of other people. How did that fit into this situation? And what about trusting God for the grace to do what I was being asked to do?

In retrospect, I know the prayer I prayed was Romans 8:26-27 in action--I didn't know what to pray but the Holy Spirit interceded through me. "Father," I said, "is this a *speaking the truth in love* (Ephesians 4:15) "I can't do this" time, or a "My grace is sufficient for you" (II Corinthians 12:9) time?" Throughout that the next two days, I either heard or read II Corinthians 12:9 three or more times. I knew God was saying His strength would be made perfect in my weakness; He would enable me to do what would otherwise have been impossible.

So by faith, I accepted the conversational English class schedule. (I believe they did rearrange the ages of the children's classes somewhat so that I only had three children's classes back to back instead of four.) Every Wednesday I taught two hour-long English classes in the morning at a church, three high-energy children's classes in the afternoon at another church, and two hour-long English classes in our home on Thursday morning. And every week, as I looked to God for grace, His strength was made perfect in my weakness. I was amazed at the energy that flowed through me, especially on Wednesdays which was a marathon for me.

All of that said, I believe far too many of us simply add more and more activities to our schedule, especially ministry activities, assuming that God wants us to say "yes," because we're doing *His* work. But I don't believe it's God's plan that we try to live outside the constraints of time, getting only a few hours of sleep and neglecting our families on a regular basis. One of my daily calendars by Cynthia Heald stated that most of our temptations and testings come not from the temptation to do evil but from the temptation to do things which are in themselves good, but interfere with our walk with God, family or other responsibilities.

We're told that the Proverbs 31 woman, *considers a [new] field before she buys or accepts it [expanding prudently and not courting neglect of her present duties by assuming other duties];* (Proverbs 31:16 AMPC).

How important it is to make sure any changes we're considering are part of God's plan for us. Only then can we assume that His grace will be sufficient for us.

Thank you, Father, for your amazing grace
that is made perfect in our weakness. Help us to discern your plan so
that we don't say "no" to difficult things you've asked us to do or yes to
things that aren't your will. Amen.

OUR PART
February 2

I've mentioned before that I have fibromyalgia. Those of you who understand that condition can imagine that finding ways to keep pain levels in check was one of my main concerns in going to Japan for a year in 2003. In the United States, going to a massage therapist was one of the methods I used, but how to find a therapist in Japan? Learning to depend more and more on the One who knows all things, I prayed, "Lord, if you want me to continue having massage therapy in Japan, guide me to the right person."

A few days later, I met a blonde, blue-eyed woman on the bike path near our home. Julie was from the Ukraine but spoke some English. When she told me she was a physical trainer, I asked if she knew of anyone who did massage therapy. She said, "I just came from a place where they do something similar. Come, I'll take you there." We walked to a small clinic about ten minutes from our house. Julie introduced me to Dr. Shiroto who did acupuncture and acupressure therapy. The fee they charged me was so low (300 Yen after National Insurance's share—about $3), I was able to have acupressure therapy every week. Dr. Shiroto was so skillful that I had one of the most pain-free years ever.

When I went for one of my last visits, Dr. Shiroto told me that he was moving his business to Aomori (a prefecture in northern Japan more than 350 miles from Tokyo) where his father, a medical doctor, lived. He would leave a day or two after my return to the United States in 2004! My heart overflowed with gratitude to God that Dr. Shiroto wasn't leaving until I no longer needed him.

A wonderful postscript to this story came when we went on a prayer trip to northern Japan in 2007. Stephen Dupree, another missionary with our mission organization, accompanied us, and we met Dr. Shiroto and his wife and son for lunch in Aomori. I had never met his wife, Tomoyo, so when I said something to her in English, Stephen started to translate into Japanese. In perfect English, she said, "Oh, you don't need to translate for me." We discovered Tomoyo had lived in the United States for some years and had taught kindergarten here.

Tomoyo and I became good friends and have kept in touch through Facebook since our return to the United States. Her family has had some significant challenges for which we've been privileged to pray. She bought my book, Homespun Faith, when it became available on Amazon Japan. I'm still in awe of how God brought us together because of my need for massage therapy.

When we returned to Japan for three years in 2008, I began having problems with my hip that made it impossible for me to stand for more than a few minutes. Finally one of my friends from another mission asked me what I was going to do about this problem. I said, "If I were in the United States, I'd go to a chiropractor, but I don't know any chiropractors here."

She said, "I do! He's a Christian and he has a special missionary rate because National Insurance doesn't cover chiropractic."

I discovered this chiropractor not only had trained in the United States and spoke English, the method he used was a combination of massage and chiropractic! His office was an easy walk from a train line that came from Higashimurayama where we lived, so I was able to go there by myself when necessary. This chiropractic method was so successful that I didn't need massage therapy.

Why was I surprised that once again God had provided exactly what I needed? This reminds me of a Veggie Tale's song: *My God is so big, so strong and so mighty, there's nothing my God cannot do*! Fibromyalgia was no match for God!

Do you have any seemingly insurmountable obstacles in your life? Through the incidents I described today and many others, Donn and I are learning that our part is to do what God asks of us. His part is to supply all our needs according to His riches in Christ Jesus (Philippians 4:19 NIV). Have you done your part?

Thank you, Jesus, for your promise that when we seek *first* your Kingdom and your righteousness, all these things shall be added to us (Matthew 6:33). Amen.

IT'S MY BALL!
February 20

Last week we babysat five-year-old, boy/girl twins* for a friend. One of them wanted to play with a small basketball he'd found. Not sure what my friend's rules were, I told Tyler* he could only roll, not throw, the ball in the house. He cocked his head and said defiantly, "It's MY ball, and I can do with it what I want!" Every time I warned him about throwing the ball, he repeated his mantra.

Somehow Tyler's words had a familiar ring which I couldn't place at first. Then it came to me. This is basically the philosophy and argument of those who say that a woman has a *right* to have an abortion: "It's MY body, and I can do with it what I want."

While I don't condone abortions for non-Christians, I am mystified by Christians who have this philosophy. I Corinthians 6:19-20 says to believers, "Do you not know that your bodies are temples of the Holy Spirit, who is in you, whom you have received from God? *You are not your own; you were bought at a price.* Therefore honor God with your bodies." If you're a follower of Jesus Christ, your body is NOT your own--it belongs to Him.

The Apostle Paul adds in Romans 12:1, *Therefore, I urge you, brothers and sisters, in view of God's mercy, to offer your bodies as a living sacrifice, holy and pleasing to God...* Bodies that have been offered to God as living sacrifices do not belong to us. Paul goes on to say, *Don't be conformed to the pattern of this world.* The pattern of this world is to avoid anything that could be the least bit uncomfortable or unpleasant--carrying a baby for nine months, going through labor and delivery, paying all the expenses that raising a child entails.

In two of the Gospels, Jesus said, *Whoever wants to be my disciple must deny themselves and take up their cross and follow me* (Matthew 16:24, Like 9:23). We live in a culture that knows little about self-denial. Christians and non-Christians alike indulge their appetites for pre-marital or extra-marital sex, and when a baby results, are unwilling to *deny themselves* in whatever ways are necessary to give that baby life.

Unless the pregnancy is the result of rape, we had a choice whether or not we would have sex. If pregnancy results, we have a choice whether or not to have an abortion. However, in either case, we cannot control the outcome. There is forgiveness for the sin of having sex outside of marriage and there is forgiveness for the sin of abortion, but a lifetime filled with regret often follows. How much better to surrender our bodies to God and make choices using His Word as our standard, rather than our culture.

Forgive us, Father, when we refuse to acknowledge as Christians that our bodies belong to you. Forgive us when we buy into the philosophy of our culture. Pour out your Spirit and restore us to righteousness by the renewing of our minds. Amen.

I'M CALLING
March 2

Last Tuesday the promise on my World Challenge calendar was Psalm 50:15. Picking up my pen, I journaled the forty-year-old memory it brought back. As a child, our blond, blue-eyed son, Robbie, had a serious problem with eczema on the back of his knees. Eventually, we ran out of the very expensive ointment our doctor had prescribed and money was tight. Donn and I were just learning the basics of claiming God's promises and seriously praying for healing, so although our default mode was to call the doctor, I told Donn I thought we should pray first.

That night as we prepared to have our devotional time together, Donn picked up our Living Bible and said, "Give me a number between one and a hundred." Baffled, I stared at him but he didn't elaborate. "Fifty," I replied. He turned to the fiftieth Psalm and began to read. Verse 15 was in italics: *I want you to trust me in your times of trouble, so I can rescue you and you can give me glory.*

"That's it," I exclaimed, "that's our promise to claim for Robbie's eczema!" Our son was already in bed, but the next day, Donn and I laid hands on him and prayed, claiming Psalm 50:15 for the healing of his skin condition. It was not an instantaneous miracle but day by day his condition improved, and within a few weeks, the irritated skin was completely healthy.

I needed to be reminded of that promise last week and I meditated on the NIV rendering: *Call upon me in the day of trouble and I will deliver you and you will honor me.* There were many situations in many arenas that troubled me, so I wrote in my journal, "I'm calling on you, Father, for every situation that troubles me." I listed them.

When I finished, I turned to the next scripture reference that accompanied the In Touch devotional I use: John 14:26-27 Amplified. Again the verses were familiar: *Peace I leave with you...Not as the world gives do I give to you. Do not let your hearts be troubled, neither let them be afraid. [Stop allowing yourselves to be agitated and disturbed; and do not permit yourselves to be fearful and intimidated and cowardly and unsettled.]* (Amplified) I asked God to help me choose His peace and choose not to be troubled or afraid.

The week went on and Saturday night I slept little. In the dark hours, I began to worry about all the situations I'd called on God about, plus a few more. So like the children of Israel, I forgot all of the deliverances and miracles of the past and all the promises we've claimed. I felt miserable and impotent as I focused on the issues that troubled me.

Sunday afternoon I picked up our electronic tablet, opened a book,* and looked at the title of the next chapter, "Giving Your Troubles to God." You'd think that might have jogged my memory but it wasn't until I reached the section called, "Giving it Up," that I really started paying attention: *So what's in your hand? Is that worry, burdens, heartache, pain, and fear I see? Why are you lugging that around? What if you knew someone wanted to carry these burdens for you?*

The author referenced Matthew 11:28-30 (*Come to me, all you who are weary and burdened, and I will give you rest...*) and I Peter 5:7 (*Give all your worries and cares to God, for He cares about you.*) Then she said, "Perhaps it's time to trust the Lord. If you're ready to hand over your burdens, pray this along with me:

"Dear Lord, I'm ready to let go. I'm ready to give up control of my burdens. From now on, these burdens ___________________________
are yours. I give them to you to carry. While we're at it, would you worry about them for me? I give you permission to come up with your own solutions. These burdens no longer belong to me, they belong to you. For you say in your Word, Call upon me in the day of trouble; I will deliver you, and you will honor me" (Psalm 50:15).
I'm calling on you now.
In the name of Jesus and by the power of his name and resurrection power, I pray, Amen."

I'm happy to say my memory kicked in full force when I saw Psalm 50:15. I went back and looked at my journal from the previous week and repented for taking everything back that I'd called on the Lord about. Then I prayed and wrote down Linda Evans Shepherd's prayer (above), giving last week's burdens to God again, plus the new

*"When You Can't Find God, How to Ignite the Power of His Presence" by Linda Evans Shepherd.

ones I'd added. Now every time one of those situations comes to mind, I just whisper, "I'm calling, Lord. I'm calling."

What about you? Are you carrying heavy burdens that our Heavenly Father wants to carry for you? Is it time for you to trust God and hand over your burdens to Him? If so, I encourage you to find a quiet place to pray Linda's prayer and write down all the burdens you're going to let God carry. Then when the enemy of our souls or your own imagination reminds you of them, join me in whispering, "I'm calling, Lord. I'm calling."

Even If
March 16

I've been thinking a lot lately about John the Baptist, specifically about a question he sent his followers to ask Jesus when they came to John reporting all the miracles the Messiah was doing. *Are you the one who was to come (the Messiah), or should we expect someone else?* (Matthew 11:3, Luke 7:19).

Really? Is this the same man who baptized Jesus and saw the Spirit come down from heaven and rest on Him in the form of a dove? Is this the same man who then said, *I have seen and I testify that this is the Son of God* (John 1:32-34)? And the same man who pointed at Jesus the next day and said, *Look, the Lamb of God, who takes away the sin of the world!* (John 1:29)?

It's clear from these statements that John firmly believed Jesus was the Christ, the Son of God. Yet a few chapters later, he's sending his disciples to ask Jesus if he really is the Messiah. What happened to cause John's faith to waiver? What changed?

We find the answer in Luke 3:19-20. John, who had faithfully served God and done nothing wrong, is now in prison for rebuking Herod the tetrarch for taking his brother's wife. Jesus, the one whom John thought to be the all-powerful Son of God, has done nothing to help him. And John, previously filled with faith, is now filled with doubt.

John was not the first nor will he be the last to have his faith shaken in prison, whatever that prison may be. Years ago a friend of ours, suffering with cancer, said, "If I as a human father would do everything in my power to protect my son from pain, why hasn't God healed me?" Others say they can't believe in a God who allows awful things to happen in the world.

I find Jesus' answer to John's question so interesting. First He reminds John of things he already knew: *Go and tell John the things which you hear and see: The blind see and the lame walk; the lepers are cleansed and the deaf hear; the dead are raised up and the poor have the gospel preached to them* (Matthew 11:4-5 NKJV). But then comes the word which addresses John's specific situation: *And blessed is he who is not offended because of me* (Matthew 11:6 KJV).

I believe Jesus knew intuitively that John was offended that after all he'd done for God, Jesus would allow him to remain in prison. I believe this offense allowed Satan to sow doubts in John's mind, in spite of the truth God had revealed to him on sunnier days. *Jesus must not really be the Messiah if he would allow something like this to happen to me.* Being offended, feeling hurt, angry, or insulted, by something someone has done or said, puts us in a vulnerable condition and provides fertile soil for Satan to plant his seeds.

Being offended because of something God has done or not done puts us in the most vulnerable state of all. God wants us to be honest about our feelings, to express our anger and hurt to Him. But when we begin to nurse our offense, listening to Satan's suggestions that God doesn't love us and doesn't care about us, we place ourselves in serious jeopardy.

None of us know how we will respond to the challenges God allows in our lives. Some of us may say like Peter, *Even if all fall away on account of you, I never will*, only to deny Him three times before the rooster crows. Only God knows how we will respond and only by experiencing the challenges do we discover what's in our hearts.

It became necessary for John to recognize that Jesus was still the Messiah, the Son of God, even if He didn't release John from prison, just as it becomes necessary for us to accept that God is still God even if He doesn't release us from our suffering, save our marriage, bring home our prodigal, ___________________. He is still the God who created us and loved us enough to send His Son to take the punishment for our sins so that we can spend eternity with Him. He is still the One who says, "I will never leave you nor forsake you." He is also still the One who cautions us, "Blessed is he who is not offended because of me."

The chorus of a recent song released by Mercy Me says it well: Even If...

Chorus
I know You're able and I know You can
Save through the fire with Your mighty hand
But even if You don't
My hope is You alone
I know the sorrow, and I know the hurt

Would all go away if You'd just say the word
But even if You don't
My hope is You alone

(Written by Mercy Me, David Garcia, Ben Glover, Crystal Lewis, Tim Timmons)

(Author's Note June 22, 2021)

Personally, I believe there's nothing Satan hates more than a child of God saying that even if God doesn't answer his/her prayers as they would like, they will still worship Him. In the first chapter of Job, Satan basically told God the only reason Job served Him was because God protected him and blessed him. He said if God stopped doing that, Job would curse Him to His face. Job's response when God allowed Satan to bring calamity upon him? "Though He [God] slay me, yet will I trust Him." (Job 13:15)

So when trouble comes, as it will, let's not stop asking God to heal, God to rescue, and God to intervene. But let's also not stop saying, *I know you're able and I know you can save through the fire with your mighty hand, but even if you don't,* I will remain faithful to you."

80

UNITY THROUGH COMPROMISE
March 28

I don't know how you feel about unity but I LOVE it! There's very little I love more than everyone being on the same page, getting along, and agreeing on everything. Unity seems like a terrific goal. However, last night I read in Hebrews that the name of the high priest Eliashib (Nehemiah 13) means *unity through compromise.*

Hmm... Suddenly, unity doesn't not seem like such an admirable goal after all. Although the word *compromise* can have a positive connotation (*an ability to listen to two sides in a dispute, and devise a compromise acceptable to both*), it also has a less positive meaning that has been on my mind for more than five years...*to accept standards that are lower than is desirable.*

In Nehemiah 13, we discover that Eliashib lived up to his name. David Wilkerson says, *By law, no Ammonite was permitted to set foot in the Temple. But Eliashib allowed Tobiah, an Ammonite prince, to live there. The high priest made God's house a dwelling place for a heathen!* Nehemiah tells us, "I learned about the evil thing Tobiah had done...It grieved me bitterly; therefore I threw all the household goods of Tobiah out of the room" (Nehemiah 13:7-8).

"Nehemiah was not acting on impulse or legalistic tradition. Rather, he was seeing through God's eyes, feeling as God felt, discerning the evil of the cancerous growth of compromise in God's house... O Lord, give us a body of preachers and parishioners who are sick of sin and who will take a stand against it! Give us people with enough discernment to see the depth and horror of the compromise that has crept into God's house!" (David Wilkerson)

When we returned from Japan in 2011, we began to see changes that were taking place in the body of Christ—and not for the better. Christian women in leadership were wearing low-cut tops with cleavage even on the platform, and we heard reports of people in leadership allowing unmarried couples to live in their homes. Since then, we've become aware of even more widespread compromise relating to homosexuality and abortion, to the degree that some churches have had to leave their conferences or denominations. Eventually, I asked the Lord, "What is behind these changes? What are we battling here?"

The Holy Spirit answered, "It's a spirit of compromise, the body of Christ is compromising with the culture." A counselor we visited clarified this by reading Romans 12:1-2 from The Message, *...Don't become so well-adjusted to your culture that you fit into it without even thinking... Unlike the culture around you, always dragging you down to its level of immaturity, God brings the best out of you.*

In other words, don't come into unity with the culture by compromising and lowering your standards. "The essence of compromise or mixture is to be just like the world." (David Wilkerson) In addition, because compromise is progressive, it's only a matter of time until we will lower our standards yet again.

If we are not to come into unity with the culture and with those in the church who are compromising, what should our response be? In Ezekiel 9:4, the Lord called to the man with the writing kit clothed in linen and said, *Go throughout the city of Jerusalem and put a mark on the foreheads of those who grieve and lament over all the detestable things that are done in it.*

Do you grieve and lament over all the detestable things being done in our culture, as well as in the church, or have you become so desensitized by what you read, watch, and listen to that it no longer moves you? A few years ago, a man in our small group said, "I'm going to pray that God would *re-sensitize* me to the things in our culture that are displeasing to Him so that I can do something about them." It's a wonderful prayer.

A few years ago I spoke to a manager in Walmart about a scantily clad, life-size cardboard figure of a woman in a bathing suit--in the very section where children would buy their pens and pencils for school. As the manager carried away the offensive object, she said, "If no one complains, we think it's okay." Wow! Really?

Come on, Church! If we don't even have the courage to complain to a store manager about offensive advertising, what will we do when real persecution comes? *And fear not them which kill the body, but are not able to kill the soul: but rather fear him which is able to destroy both soul and body in hell (Matthew 10:28 KJV).*

So, as I said earlier, there is very little that I love more than unity... However, there is one thing I love more... Jesus. I love Jesus, who said *I am the Truth,* more than I love unity. If the cost of having unity is accepting standards that are lower than is desirable or accepting misinterpretations of God's Word, the price is too high.

Father, your Word says, *Buy the truth and do not sell it...* (Proverbs 23:23 NIV). I pray there would never be anything or anyone we love more than the Truth so we will not be deceived. Amen.

I KNOW WHY
April 20

Many years ago I was having a lot of pain in my back. One day as I visited friends, Danielle,* a woman I'd known for a short time, said, "Let me pray for you." She put her hands on my back, prayed a short prayer, and immediately, the pain lifted.

Danielle was a professing Christian who had recently had a moral failure, and I was so puzzled that God had healed me through her prayer. On my way home, I puckered my forehead and said, "Lord, why would you choose to heal me through someone like her?" I had no doubt that Danielle was an unfit instrument.

I've never forgotten the Lord's succinct answer. "I not only know *what* people do, I know *why*."

A few days later, I talked to someone who had known Danielle for many years. She said, "I've never known anyone who has been as physically, sexually, and mentally abused as Danielle."

Suddenly God's words made sense. He looked at Danielle through eyes of compassion because He knew everything about her. In His eyes, she was doing well for someone who had been abused as she had. He knew her heart.

In some ways, I'm a pretty black and white person: right is right, and wrong is wrong. This realization that God may not see people as I do is still sometimes hard for me to comprehend. It reminds me a little of the woman who anointed Jesus with perfume from her alabaster jar in Luke 7. The Pharisee who had invited Jesus to his house definitely thought the woman wasn't worthy. He said to himself, "If this man were a prophet, he would know who is touching him and what kind of woman she is—that she is a sinner." So the assumption was that Jesus wouldn't have allowed the woman to touch Him had He known she was a sinner.

But Jesus made a habit of either touching or allowing Himself to be touched by people no one else wanted to touch—the leper he healed in Mark 1:40-42, the woman with the issue of blood in Mark 5, the

*Name has been changed.

fishermen and tax collectors he chose as his disciples. I'm sure the Scribes and Pharisees didn't think they were worthy either.

Samuel would have chosen Eliab, the handsome eldest son of Jessie, as the next king of Israel. But God said, *The Lord does not look at the things man looks at. Man looks at the outward appearance, but the Lord looks at the heart* (I Samuel 16:7 NIV).

How many times have we, like the Scribes and Pharisees, judged people as "unworthy?" How desperately we need to look at others with eyes of compassion as Jesus did, asking for the discernment of the Holy Spirit, and choosing not to disqualify people as unworthy without ever knowing their hearts.

Father, help us see others through your eyes, knowing that you not only know what people do, you know why. Amen.

LOVE MERCY
May 11

I've read Micah 6:8 more times than I can count and could probably come close to quoting it word for word:

He has shown you, O man, what is good. And what does the Lord require of you? To do justly and to love mercy and to walk humbly with your God (NIV).

But last week one portion of this verse kept coming to mind: *love mercy... love mercy... love mercy...* What does it mean to *love* mercy? Have I automatically substituted "show mercy" for "love mercy" in this scripture? Is there a difference? I think there is, though I don't fully understand it.

Over the past month or so, we've found ourselves in a situation where the Holy Spirit is prompting us to extend mercy, rather than stepping back to let someone suffer the consequences of their poor choices. While I'm cautious about doing this because, if done repeatedly, it can keep people from learning valuable lessons, I believe it's God's plan in this case. Carrying it out has included going beyond the call of duty lovingly, cheerfully... again and again and again. Saying yes with a smile when it would have been more convenient to say no. As we walk it out, I keep hearing: *love mercy.*

As I've researched the concept of loving mercy, I'm finding that much has been written about applying it to social causes, but not a great deal about applying it to our daily lives. Sometimes it's easier to apply God's Word to a "cause" than to allow Him to apply it to our hearts in ordinary situations.

As I choose to keep my heart attitude right as I go the second mile for those who may not *seem* to deserve it, I sense God's smile of approval and I come closer to understanding what it means to love mercy—or as the Contemporary English Version says, I come closer to understanding what it means to "let mercy be [my] first concern."

Father, give us hearts like yours, the One who perfectly balances doing justly and loving mercy. Enable us to walk humbly with you. Amen.

WHEN GOD RAN
(Love Mercy Part II)
May 25

In my last devotional, I talked about loving mercy (Micah 6:8) and things God is teaching me. As I explored the Scriptures for examples, I realized there's no better example than the father of the prodigal son in Jesus' parable. If anyone was undeserving of mercy, it was the prodigal son. He had shown great disrespect for his father by demanding his inheritance while his father was still alive and had gone off to squander the money in a far country.

The father's response to his son's behavior is interesting. We might expect that a father who loved mercy would go searching for the prodigal. In the past, that might have fit *my* definition of loving mercy. Instead, this mercy-loving father who knew his son well, *waited* for the inevitable to happen, waited for his son's wealth to run out, waited for his son to "come to his senses," waited for him to repent, to be ready to receive mercy.

But while he was waiting, the father never stopped watching for his son to come home. Scripture tells us that *While [the son] was still a long way off, his father saw him and was filled with compassion for him...* (Luke 15:20). Can you picture that father looking off into the distance every day, yearning to catch the first glimpse of his wayward son?

Then, even more amazing, verse 20 tells us *"[the father] ran to meet his son."* Rev. Jack Wellman says, "The Jewish culture of that day had disdain for any father who ran. Since they wore long robes, the father would have had to tuck his robe into his belt, which would have exposed his legs...This was disgraceful in that culture. A father never ran, especially to a son because the son was to honor the father." But this mercy-loving father was willing to risk disgrace in order to show mercy to his son.

Not only did the father run to his son--his son who probably smelled of pigs, an animal detestable to the Jews--but he also threw his arms around him and kissed him. At every point, the father in Jesus' parable put showing mercy to his son above the mores of Jewish culture and tradition.

Best of all, this mercy-loving father represents our mercy-loving Heavenly Father. Benny Hester's song, "When God Ran," written from the perspective of a prodigal, makes that connection. Here's the first verse and chorus: (My favorite version is by Craig Philips of Philips, Craig, and Dean on YouTube.)

Almighty God, the Great I Am, Immovable Rock,
Omnipotent, Powerful, Awesome Lord.
Victorious Warrior, Commanding King of Kings,
Mighty Conqueror and the only time,
The only time I ever saw him run,
Was when
He ran to me, He took me in His arms,
Held my head to His chest, said "My son's come home again!" Lifted my
face, wiped the tears from my eyes, with forgiveness in His voice He
said,
"Son, do you know I still love you?"
He caught me by surprise, when God ran.

Come, Holy Spirit, give us the heart of the Father. Remind us that Jesus, who was called a friend of sinners, came to show us the Father's heart. Make us like Him. Amen.

HOPING WHEN ALL HOPE IS GONE
June 5

This is how it feels to be hopeless. I identified the feeling as I stood in our dining room in Pittsburgh in 1980. I had never been hopeless before.

How had I come to this place? At the Holy Spirit's prompting, I had made a commitment to God that I would do anything He asked me to do, go anywhere He asked me to go, be anything He asked me to be (Romans 12:1). I had expected a smooth transition into whatever ministry God had for me. Instead, my life became a nightmare as I went through God's school of preparation. *Would I survive?*

My initial symptoms were physical and emotional—dizziness, sensitivity to loud noises, anger, indecisiveness, crying. When I talked to our pastor, he said, "Go home and rest, and read, and pray about the spiritual aspect of your illness."

No one had ever given me that kind of advice before, but I obeyed. Soon the Holy Spirit began a deep work. He revealed long-buried hatred, a besetting sin I'd justified, and through our pastor, the possibility of low-blood sugar. My moment of hopelessness came when my Dr. ignored my reactions to the glucose tolerance test, told me my varied and "bizarre" symptoms were "just nerves," and gave me tranquilizers.

In his chapter titled *The God of Hope*,* David Wilkerson says, "It has been said that the only thing worse than insanity is despair." I agree. The doctor to whom I'd looked to solve my problem had done his best and after taking the tranquilizers, I was much worse. I discovered that "Hopelessness is the result of trusting in man." (David Wilkerson) In the midst of my hopelessness I prayed, "Father, this doctor says my problem is just nerves, but if he's wrong, please show me."
A few days later when I picked up a pile of newspapers, a title caught my eye, "A Second Opinion, Please?" The doctor who wrote the column said that when patients whose conditions had been diagnosed as

*From David Wilkerson's book, "Hungry for More of Jesus."

"nerves" got a second opinion, it was repeatedly found that they had either low blood sugar or allergies. Hope stirred in my heart. Those were the two conditions I'd suspected I might have. I made an appointment with an allergy specialist and went to Carnegie library to read everything I could find on hypoglycemia.

According to these books, my blood sugar readings showed a classic case of hypoglycemia for a person whose blood sugar drops very rapidly even though it may not drop low enough to meet most medical doctors' criteria. From the allergy doctor, I learned that I was very allergic to molds which were rampant in our damp, finished basement.

I began to follow a high protein diet recommended by nutritionists for people with low blood sugar, receive allergy shots, and have counseling with our pastor. Gradually I began to get well. My "nerves" greatly improved! Later, when I was having a bad day, Donn prayed for me and God healed me of low blood sugar.

Please understand, I'm not opposed to doctors. We've had the same family doctor for 35 years and he's been a great blessing to us. However, I've told him more than once that the reason I appreciate him so much is because he doesn't think he's God!

It was never God's plan for us to put our hope and trust in doctors. God is the only One worthy of that. I can't imagine my condition today, physically, mentally and emotionally, if I hadn't looked to the Lord for answers, putting my hope and trust in Him alone. Many circumstances and trials may rob us of hope, but if we make God our source of hope, He will bring us through.

Now may the God of hope fill you with all joy and peace in believing, that you may abound in hope by the power of the Holy Spirit (Romans 15:13).

HOW TO BE HAPPY WITH WHAT YOU HAVE
June 20

Recently I became obsessed with finding a rug just the right size for a floor area we wanted to cover in our bedroom. However, I discovered the size rug we needed wasn't easy to find, not being a standard size. I measured several times and pictured what the different-sized rugs would look like in our bedroom. I hunted at Ollie's and online.

One day I noticed the carpet remnant on our family room floor, left over from when we'd had our upstairs carpeted four years ago. The longer I looked the more sure I became that this carpet remnant was exactly the right size for the area we wanted to cover in our bedroom. (A standard size rug would easily replace the remnant in our family room.)

When Donn and I carried the remnant to our bedroom, we found it was a perfect fit! I kept thinking of the irony of how hard we'd tried to find the perfect rug when we *already had* exactly what we needed. I wondered how often in life we do the same thing—go out searching for what we *think* we need when we already have it.

One woman I knew had been married many years to a good man but decided she wasn't happy. Eventually she left her husband and found the man she thought she wanted. Things didn't turn out well. I asked her gently, "Do you have regrets?" Sobs shook her whole body as she nodded. "So many regrets."

I read of a similar case of a woman who spent many years complaining to her calm, easy-going accountant husband *and* her friends about the unexciting life they led. When Tim died of a heart attack in his forties, Diane found the man of her dreams. He was debonair and charming, an exciting date. However, after they married, she discovered he wanted to party every night and cared little about managing finances. Later, Diane told a friend, "I wish I had married someone who was content to stay home and good at managing money." Her friend looked at her and said, "Someone like Tim?" God had given her exactly what she needed, but she'd been too blind to appreciate him.

This reminds me of two of my favorite children's books: *Old*

Hat, New Hat and *The Best Nest*. The moral of each story is the same. In *Old Hat, New Hat* the bear sets out to buy a new hat. He tries on or looks at 31 different hats, but finds something wrong with each one. (Do you remember? "Too big. Too small. Too flat. Too tall. etc.") In the end, he puts on his old hat, looks in the mirror and says, "Just right! Just right. Just right. Just right." He leaves the store wearing his old hat with a smile on his face.

In *The Best Nest*, Mr. Bird loves their nest and sings often, "I love my house. I love my nest. In all the world, my nest is best!" Mrs. Bird has a different opinion of their nest, but in the end, after looking at many other nests, Mrs. Bird also realizes that the nest they have is, after all, the best nest.

Old Hat, New Hat and *The Best Nest* have happy endings because the creatures came to appreciate what they already had. However, in the real world, as in the other two stories I shared, the endings aren't always happy. We may leave a marriage, a job, a house, or any number of places or situations, and later, when we realize the value of what we had, we discover it's too late.

Charles Stanley recently said many people love to quote Psalm 37:4 (*Delight yourself in the Lord and He will give you the desires of your heart*), but fail to understand that the promise has a condition we must fulfill. Psalm 90:14 says, "Satisfy me early with your love that I may delight in you all the day." As the Lord becomes our delight, He aligns our desires with His.

If we find ourselves unhappy and dissatisfied with our marriage, our job, our church, our home, perhaps the first step shouldn't be to look for a new man/woman, job, church, home. Perhaps the first step should be to ask God to satisfy us with His love so that we can delight in Him and trust Him to give us the desires of our hearts. In many cases, we may discover that He already has.

Father, forgive us for trying so hard
to find what we want that we're blinded to the fact that you've often
already given us what we need. Amen.

HE CAME TO HIMSELF
June 22

I talked recently about hoping when all hope is gone. Today I'd like to talk a little more about hopelessness. I was hopeless because a doctor I'd depended on had failed to find the solution to my illness, and had, in fact, led me to believe my problem was "just nerves." However, there are many other reasons people may feel hopeless—a bad marriage, a terminal health condition, a prodigal son or daughter, financial problems, an addiction, and many more.

Charles Stanley says personal failure is also a thief of hope. This certainly applies to the prodigal son, out of money in a foreign country experiencing a severe famine. He was so desperate he hired himself out to feed pigs, a particularly demeaning position for a Jew. His hunger was so strong that even the pigs' food looked good. Hopelessness must have been his constant companion.

But it was in this hopeless situation that we're told the prodigal "came to himself," or "came to his senses." Andrew Breeden of The Upper Room says, "Few words give me more hope than those four. The prodigal came to himself. The more I sit with the story, the more compelled I am by the beauty of the prodigal's revelation while feeding the pigs—that moment when something gone quite awry became the grace that saved him. And this brings me hope—for myself and for everyone...The point of the story is that there is hope. No matter the pigpen I am in, *I can come to myself.*"

I love the words of the prodigal in verse 18 of Luke 15, *I will arise and go to my father...*" When the wayward son came to his senses, he knew where to go! He might have said, as people sometimes do, "I brought it all on myself. I can't expect my father (God) to help me now." But instead, he arose and went to his father with words of repentance—and received far better than he deserved. He was restored to his position as a son!

While hopeless situations may seem like the end of the world, they may actually be the beginning. They can be the incentive we need to "come to our senses." They can be the agent of change that prompts us to "arise and go to our Father" with words of repentance on our lips. He is longing to restore us to our position as sons and daughters of His.

Whatever pigpen I find myself in today, I will arise and go to my Father.

OUTSIDE THE CAMP
July 13

We've been hearing a lot lately at our church about forgiveness. A few weeks ago, our pastor preached on loving our enemies, Matthew 5:43-48. I'd like to think that everyone in our church gets along and no one harbors ill will against anyone. At the same time, I realize that's probably a fantasy. The enemy loves to sow seeds of discord in churches and Christian organizations, yours and mine.

But here's my point: We may think our disagreement with someone in our church or organization, our refusal to speak to them, our ill will toward them, our refusal to let go of our offense, only affects the two of us. We may think it's really no one else's affair, no one else's business. But what if our sin of unforgiveness is interfering with what God wants to do in our church/organization/family? What if our portion of the body of Christ can't go forward until the offense has been forgiven, the wound has been healed, the relationship has been restored? None of us sin in a vacuum, and I Corinthians 12:26 says if one part of the body suffers, every part suffers.

As Pastor Nathan encouraged us to forgive our enemies and love one another, I remembered an Old Testament incident involving Moses' sister, Miriam. We're told in Numbers 12 she was stricken with leprosy because she and her brother, Aaron, spoke against Moses. Aaron immediately interceded for her with Moses, and Moses interceded for her with God. God said Miriam would have to stay outside the camp for seven days.

The next verse is the one I can't stop thinking about. *So Miriam was confined outside the camp for seven days, and the people did not move on till she was brought back* (Numbers 12:14). Not only was *Miriam* affected by the consequences of her sin, but no one in the Israelite camp could move on until her condition was healed. The entire group was affected.

We're told in Mark 11:25, *If you have aught against any, forgive... Aught* means anything at all, even the smallest thing. I'm asking God to search our hearts and reveal to us if we're holding anything against anyone, if our unwillingness to forgive is keeping the body of Christ from going forward, from growing spiritually into the image of Christ. If you want to forgive but feel something is hindering you, reach out to someone you trust and ask them to pray that the Holy Spirit would enable you to forgive.

Father, help us recognize the widespread effect of our sin of unforgiveness. Help us choose to forgive so the body of Christ isn't hindered. Amen.

Unoffendable?
July 26

The day before I was to post my already-finished blog on forgiveness (Outside the Camp), I talked to a friend who had been treated unkindly. After we talked at some length about her quandary as to how to handle the situation, I said, "You know, eventually you will have to forgive her." I shared some of the words from our pastor's last message and prayed with her.

Over the next few days, the Holy Spirit brought two people to my mind, and I realized I'd been upset with them for some time. Each time He whispered, "You know, eventually you will have to forgive him/her." I remembered that near the end of my blog, I'd said, "I'm asking God to search our hearts and reveal to us if we're holding anything against anyone..." Wow! He had taken me at my word.

A day or two later, I picked up a folder that contained various messages or articles I'd saved thinking I'd reread the messages "sometime." When I opened the folder, the first message was titled, "How To Become Unoffendable" by Francis Frangipane. I wondered, as I had when I'd read this message before, if this is even possible...to become unoffendable? Then I remembered a favorite verse from Psalm 119:165, (KJV), *Great peace have they which love Thy law, and **nothing** shall offend them.*

Frangipane says, "People don't usually stumble over boulders, they stumble over stones--relatively small things. It may be that the personality of someone in authority bothers us, and soon, we are offended. Or, a friend or family member fails to meet our expectations, and we take an offense into our soul...The occasions for taking offense are practically endless. Indeed, we are daily given the opportunity to either be offended or to possess an unoffendable heart."

The next message in my folder was titled, "Forgiveness," and written as though the Lord is speaking. (I have no author's name for this.)

"I understand you were offended and it hurt. Let Me bring the pain to the surface and cleanse it from any infection. I know it is difficult, but the only way to preserve your own freedom from this offense is to forgive. Whether the offense was intentional or not, to nurse your feelings will only cause the wound to grow and become infected.

"Unforgiveness binds the soul and keeps the offense fresh in the mind and heart. Over and over again the enemy will bring it to memory and build upon it, expanding its pain by resurrecting other offenses...This causes an even greater gap between yourself and that person...When you release someone from offense, you release yourself as well."

If God's Word says that *nothing* will offend those who love His law, then I know it must be possible to be unoffendable. However, until I have attained that state, I want to be quick to forgive when I realize I am offended. I love Francis Frangipane's closing prayer:

"Lord, forgive me for being so easily offended and for carrying offenses. My heart is foolish and weak, Father. Grant me the unoffendable heart of Jesus Christ. Amen."

"People who want to live powerful lives must become experts at forgiving those who offend and hurt them." (Author unknown)

DECEPTION
August 11

I've been thinking a lot lately about deception—how it happens, why it happens, especially to Christians. Webster says "to deceive is to cause (someone) to believe something that is not true." Hmmm... This definition begins with the assumption that there is such a thing as truth.

At a high school reunion years ago, one of my classmates asked me, "What is truth?" In a culture that is prone to say, "My truth is not your truth and your truth isn't necessarily my truth" that can be difficult to define. However, Jesus said in his prayer in John 17:17, "Sanctify them by the truth; your Word is truth" (NIV).

If God's Word is truth, then why can't Christians agree in our present culture war? Could it be that deception is more widespread in the church than ever before, causing the present divide? Recently, Donn and I talked to a man who had been my pastor for years and who performed our marriage ceremony in the Mennonite church. As we discussed events taking place not only in that denomination but in many others, Donn said, "But how can Christians believe these things (about homosexuality) in light of what the Bible teaches?"

My former pastor said with more than a hint of irony, "They say we have somehow misinterpreted Romans 1 all these years! They also say that the sin of Sodom was not homosexuality but lack of hospitality." I knew he was right, but still I wondered, *How did it happen?* How could people who once knew and stood for the truth be so totally deceived?

And yet we need only go to the book of Genesis for the answer. In Genesis 3:1 we find the first reference to the enemy of our souls twisting God's Words. "*Did God really say, 'You must not eat from any tree in the garden*?'" Of course that's *not* what God said, but Satan was trying to portray God as a killjoy who wouldn't allow them to eat from *any* of the trees in the garden. After Eve gave her own rendition of twisting God's Word, the serpent went even further, twisting God's Word to an even greater degree.

Eve had the same choice each of us have when confronted with a twisted version of Scripture—she could either choose to believe God or choose to believe Satan. Why did she choose to believe Satan? Why do we choose to believe him?

In Eve's case it's clear she wanted to eat the apple because it looked good and she thought it would taste good and make her wise. Could the same be true today? To Christians who have same sex attractions, the person to whom they're attracted looks good. Having sex with them sounds enjoyable.

In addition, if someone has given these people the twisted version of God's Word, there is the added appeal of being wiser than those who have "misinterpreted" the Bible all these years. The people they're listening to usually aren't painting a clear picture of the emotional and physical liabilities of the lesbian/homosexual lifestyle.

It's much easier to sin if we have convinced ourselves first that what we want to do isn't wrong. In 2010 Donn told me one of our favorite Christian singers was now saying he is gay. I immediately did a Google search to discover which stance he was taking: *I know this is wrong, but I don't care*, or *I no longer believe homosexuality is wrong*. The answer was clear—he is now part of a church which embraces homosexuality. I wept and grieved over this man for days.

In her book *Uninvited,* Lisa Terkeurst says, "I had truth. But I had not applied the truth. Therefore, my mind did what my feelings wanted. The decision in that moment was made with a mind conformed to what seemed acceptable to the world. It was not a mind transformed by truth...[I thought] trading God's truth for what the world said was a better plan...What started off as a seemingly small compromise can easily become a complete contradiction to the people we long to be...Only when we seek to apply Jesus' revelations to our situations will we experience transformation."

So it is not truth that protects us from deception, but truth applied to our situation. May God grant us wisdom to understand the difference. In my next devotional, we'll talk about Adam and the reason he, and many like him, was deceived.

Father, forgive us for becoming so well-adjusted to our culture that we fit into it without even thinking. Help us apply your teachings to our lives in a way that protects us from deception. Amen.

Don't become so well-adjusted to your culture that you fit into it without

*even thinking. Instead, fix your attention on God. You'll be changed
from the inside out. Readily recognize what he wants from you, and
quickly respond to it. Unlike the culture around you, always dragging
you down to its level of immaturity, God brings the best out of you,
develops well-formed maturity in you (Romans 12:2 The Message).*

Deception
PART II
August 18

In Part I, we talked about deception, about how Eve's deception may be similar to the deception of some Christians who have same sex attractions. How Satan twisted God's Word then and now. In Part II I want to talk about Adam, how and why he was deceived. Why he ate of the fruit.

Could it be that Adam loved the beautiful creature God had given him so much that he didn't want to refuse the fruit she offered him or do anything to "cause trouble in paradise?" Could it be this is why he too chose to eat the fruit, opening the door to the worst trouble that could be imagined and bringing an end to paradise as he knew it? Could it be that he wanted to please Eve more than he wanted to please God? I've heard it said if we love anything or anyone more than the truth, we will be deceived.

This is similar to how I believe the Adam syndrome might work today in relation to Christians being deceived about homosexuality. Someone tells their Christian family/friends that they're gay. Gradually, one by one other members of their family/friends begin to embrace the new philosophies about homosexuality.

This might happen because: 1) elderly parents are financially dependent on the person who is in the same sex relationship; 2) the family/friends are afraid of losing relationship with that person and they can't bear the thought of a rift in the family; 3) someone whom they trust or who has more education than they, has embraced the new philosophy; 4) or they themselves have a high level of compassion and they can't bear to have their friend/family member who is gay or even homosexuals/lesbians in general feel rejected. In any case, they too choose to believe a lie.

Some time ago I learned that the wife of a well-known Christian speaker believed in gay marriage. Later, I wasn't surprised to hear that the speaker himself had changed his views on homosexuality. I also read an article a few years later about the wife of the singer I mentioned last week. She said she knew if she held to the older views of homosexuality—that it's wrong and offensive to God, she would lose her (now ex-) husband as a friend. Since then I've read that she is an advocate for Soulforce, a pro-gay group that fights for gay rights. Perhaps one of the ways we open ourselves to deception is by making idols out of those we love, those we think we can't live without.

Could it be that when we want to please others more than we want to please God, we become willing to trade the truth of God for a lie? Romans 1:25-27 NIV says:

They traded the truth about God for a lie. So they worshiped and served the things God created instead of the Creator Himself, who is worthy of eternal praise! That is why God abandoned them to their shameful desires. Even the women turned against the natural way to have sex and instead indulged in sex with each other. And the men, instead of having normal sexual relations with women, burned with lust for each other. Men did shameful things with other men, and as a result of this sin, they suffered within themselves the penalty they deserved. Since they thought it foolish to acknowledge God, He abandoned them to their foolish thinking and let them do things that should never be done.

I believe our greatest protection against deception is loving Jesus more than anything or anyone else and loving His Word, being alert for any attempts of the enemy to twist its meaning. When Satan came to tempt Jesus in the wilderness, Jesus answered him using God's Word, *It is written...* In his third temptation, Satan tried to turn the tables on Jesus by using Scripture to entice Him to sin, but Jesus spotted his wrong use of Scripture and corrected him with one last, *It is written...* Will we let the Holy Spirit help us do the same or will II Thessalonians 2:11-12 NIV become true of us?

They perish because they refused to love the truth and so be saved. For this reason God sends them a powerful delusion so that they will believe the lie and so that all will be condemned who have not believed the truth but have delighted in wickedness.

Father, Enable us to *Love you with all of our hearts, souls, strength, and minds* (Luke 10:27), and to *Buy the truth and sell it not...* (Proverbs 23:23). Help us remember that *Your Word is Truth* (John 17:17) so that it will be *a lamp to our feet and a light for our path* (Psalm 119:105). Amen.

PROBLEM AT THE TOP OF THE STAIRS
September 12

Do not worry or be anxious about tomorrow, for tomorrow will have worries and anxieties of its own. Sufficient for each day is its own trouble. (Matthew6:34AMPC)

Before we moved into our house in Greenville, we worried a lot because there was no door at the top of the basement stairs —just a short hallway between the top of the basement stairs and the open doorway into the kitchen. We were sure cold air from the basement would creep up the steps, making the kitchen chilly in the winter. Over and over we discussed different options to take care of this potential problem. Or maybe it just seemed like over and over because I thought so much about it, trying to come up with solutions.

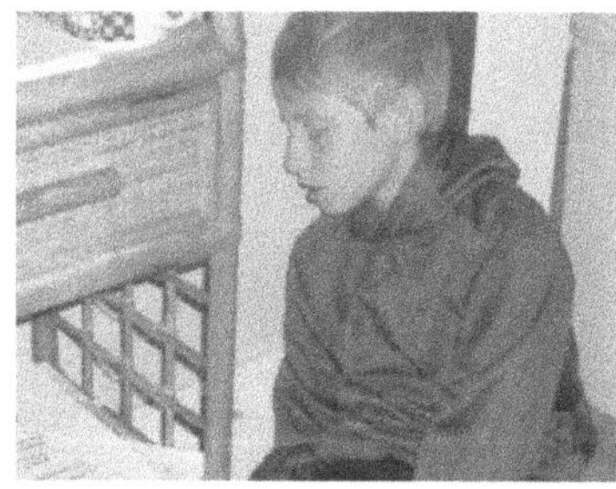

When we moved into our home two and a half months later, we discovered that the lack of a door at the top of the basement stairs wasn't a problem at all. The register in the kitchen, a direct run from the basement, was the best in the house, and our grandson, Connor often went there to get warm on winter mornings! None of the solutions we'd discussed were necessary. We'd spent all that time and energy trying to fix a problem that never materialized.

The other day as I fretted and stewed about a situation over which I have no control and the problems to which it might lead, I remembered the no-kitchen-door scenario. Having now lived in this house for six years, I shook my head at how much time and energy we'd wasted on something that *might* be a problem. Matthew 6:34 came to mind...today has enough of its own problems without worrying about the ones that might come tomorrow.

The next day my daily calendar contained this wisdom:

Beloved, you will never find security by trying to anticipate all the storms that may reach you someday. Remember that I control the atmosphere of your life. Trust Me by relaxing and releasing your concerns into My capable care. It saddens Me to see you obsessing about possible problems, rather than bringing these matters to Me. When you find yourself anxiously scanning the horizon of your life, use that as a reminder to seek My face...

Instead of wasting time worrying, devote that time to developing close friendship with Me...Ask me to lift your perspective from a problem-focus to a Presence-focus. Remember that I am holding you by your right hand. I guide you with My counsel, based on eternal wisdom; so there's no need to worry about the future...Your best refuge in life's storms is close friendship with Me. (Dear Jesus by Sarah Young)

(Author's Note November 4, 2020)

The present conditions in our country--the pandemic, the rioting and racial unrest, the election--make it seem impossible NOT to worry about tomorrow. In times like these, we need a minute by minute decision to trust. Those words remind me of a song made popular by George Beverly Shea:

In times like these you need a Savior,
In times like these you need an anchor;
Be very sure, be very sure,
Your anchor holds and grips the Solid Rock!

This Rock is Jesus, Yes He's the One,
This Rock is Jesus, the only One;
Be very sure, be very sure,
Your anchor holds and grips the Solid Rock!

So here's my prayer request for today—feel free to make it your own:

Father, lift my perspective from a problem-focus to a Presence-focus. Help me keep my eyes fixed on you rather than peering into the distance, looking for potential problems. Amen.

LONGINGS
October 5

Sometime ago, a devotional titled, *Your Heart's Desire,* spoke to me. Here are a few excerpts:

When we delight in the Lord, He gives us the desire of our heart. If we delight in financial success, washboard abs, or highly accomplished children, He makes no promises....

Take an honest look at the things you long for, dream about and desire. What do they reveal about your relationship with God? What, if any, changes do you need to make?

So I took an honest look at the things I long for, dream about and desire. I discovered that financial success, washboard abs, or highly accomplished children weren't even at the bottom of my list! I can't even say I *long* for my new book to be published, although it's something I want. Here are a few of the longings at the top of my list:

I long for all our children and their spouses to be men/women of God who value Him and a holy life above all else, who tenderly guide their families and treat them with dignity and respect, and who are faithful to their mates in every thought and deed.

I long for all our grandchildren to be boys/girls, men/women, of God who love God with all their hearts, souls, strength and minds., who are pure in heart and mind, rejecting the culture's wicked ways, and who keep their word, especially to God and their family.

I long for our family to want to visit us, to want to spend time with us, to want to be together.

I wrote down many more longings that day but as I read the first ones, I realized perhaps they weren't too different from the longings God has for His children, His family. He *longs* for us to be men and women of God who lead holy lives and love Him with all our hearts, souls, minds, and strength. He longs for us to spend time with Him because we *want* to, not as a duty, and He longs for us to want to spend time with each other, our brothers and sisters in Christ.

During our church's worship night on Sunday evening, I realized that although there was nothing *wrong* with my longings, Psalm 63:1 revealed an even deeper longing God wanted me to have. *You, God, are my God, earnestly I seek you; I thirst for you, my whole being longs for you, in a dry and parched land where there is no water.* I knew I couldn't honestly say that my *whole being* longs for God.

When God created Adam and Eve, He set the stage for those He loves to reject or ignore His desire for intimacy. Just as I can't force our children and grandchildren to long for a closer relationship with me, God will not force us to long to be closer to Him. He won't force us to put Him first or love Him most or spend time with Him. One of our children asked me years ago, "How can we love God, whom we cannot see, more than we love our children who are so dear to us?" It's a difficult question.

While I knew I couldn't honestly say the words of Psalm 63:1 on Sunday evening, I knew I *wanted* to be able to say them. Later, I read a prayer on Instagram by A. W. Tozer that expressed the desire of my heart. Would you read it aloud and let the Holy Spirit do what only He can do?

O God, I have tasted Thy goodness, and it has both satisfied me and made me thirsty for more. I am painfully conscious of my need of further grace. I am ashamed of my lack of desire. O God, the Triune God, I want to want Thee; I long to be filled with longing; I thirst to be made more thirsty still. Show me Thy glory, I pray Thee, so I may know Thee indeed. Begin in mercy a new work of love within me. Say to my soul, 'Rise up, my love, my fair one, and come away.' Then give me grace to rise and follow Thee up from this.

Father, even though we may not be able to say with the
Psalmist that our whole being longs for you, we can say with A. W.
Tozer that we *want* to want you, we *long* to be filled with longing, we
thirst to be made more thirsty still. We invite you, Holy Spirit, to create
in us what we are unable to create in ourselves. Amen.

BUT AFTERWARD...
October 9

In my book, Homespun Faith, I told how the Lord provided a way to keep our lovely upright piano in the family when we went to Japan. My sisters and I had helped my dad refinish this piano, so it had a lot of sentimental value. When our daughter, Angelyn, took the piano, she started asking questions about the history of this beautiful piece of furniture.

I asked for input from my older siblings since I'm next to the youngest of seven. My oldest sister, Lucy, told me the story. Mom had noticed Lucy had musical ability, heard her playing musical instruments in other people's homes. So she asked Daddy if we could buy a piano. He agreed. Since there was never much money for extras, Mom asked how much we could spend. He told her $25.

Lucy told me Mom had done what she did best--she prayed, asking God for a piano for $25. Sometime near Lucy's 16th birthday, Daddy came home from the filling station saying he'd heard someone had a piano available for $25 if he would come and get it. He made arrangements and our family became the owners of an upright piano covered in less-than- attractive black stain.

No one remembers exactly when the huge stripping process began, maybe around 1968. We used everything imaginable, including toothbrushes, to remove the black stain and reveal the beautiful designs on the book rest. When at last the piano was stripped and lightly stained, the transformation was breathtaking. The piano was almost unrecognizable as the one Daddy had purchased for $25.

I can't help but compare this process to the Holy Spirit's ability to strip away the things that hinder our beauty from shining through the black stain of self and sin. To the world, we may not appear valuable, but our Heavenly Father knows the masterpiece hidden under the stain because He Himself created it! Sometimes the stripping process is painful, but afterward, it's worth it all. The words "but afterward" always remind me of Hebrews 12:11: *No discipline is enjoyable while it is happening—it's painful!* **But afterward** *there will be a peaceful harvest of right living for those who are trained in this way (NLT).*

Father, when we're going through a painful stripping process, help us fix our eyes on Jesus and the *But afterward* that will make it all worthwhile. Amen.

Photos: 1) My sister, Ruth, and me in 1967. 2) Our granddaughter, Joy, in 2008.

IS IT POSSIBLE TO LOVE OUR ENEMIES?
December 7

Of all the "hard sayings" of Jesus in the Sermon on the Mount, perhaps one of the most difficult is His instruction to love our enemies. Years ago, I had a co-worker who treated me badly. One day I congratulated myself on the fact that I'd never been unkind to her, never returned evil for evil and never tried to get even. Then the Holy Spirit whispered, "But you don't love her." He was SO right, and I stood stripped of all my "righteousness" in God's presence. Even though I had refrained from taking revenge, my heart wasn't right.

Sometimes we wonder how it is even possible to love our enemies. What does that look like? Romans 12:20-21 says: *"If your enemy is hungry, feed him; if he is thirsty, give him something to drink. In doing this, you will heap burning coals on his head.* (v. 21) *Do not be overcome by evil, but overcome evil with good (NIV)."* I believe verse 21 is the key--overcoming evil with good.

The best example I've ever seen of this came from a young woman I'll call Cindy. She had suffered a great deal at the hands of one of the older players on her basketball team whom I'll call Marsha. Cindy was an excellent player and Marsha felt that Cindy had robbed her of a starting role on the team. But no matter what Marsha did, Cindy continued to treat her with kindness.

A week or two before the night when seniors are honored, Cindy told her mother, "I think it would mean a lot to Marsha to be one of the starters on senior night. I'm going to ask the coach to put her in my starting position for that game." Later, as we watched the game, we saw Cindy give Marsha a sincere hug, when she was being honored, and more than polite applause. I sent Cindy the following note, "There'll come a time when your athletic ability won't be so important, but character is forever!"

I believe one of the clearest indicators that we are fulfilling Jesus' commandment to love our enemies is when we not only refrain from doing anything to hurt them but we also make every effort to do things for them that are good. It may even be that as we go the extra mile to do those good things, God Himself does the impossible, filling our hearts with love for them.

Father, enable us to obey your command to love our enemies in tangible ways so that you can fill our hearts with your love. Amen.

THE ROCKS WOULD CRY OUT
December 27

I mentioned before that one of our favorite American contemporary Christian singers made choices that broke my heart. I grieved for months. How could someone as solid as we'd thought this singer was in his faith make the choices he was making? What hope was there if someone like that had fallen?

This happened while we were in Japan, and I expressed these thoughts to our OMS Regional Director, Bill Oden, who was visiting the Japan field at the time. He responded, "I have yet seven thousand in Israel who have not bowed their knee to Baal." (I Kings 19:18)

I replied, "You're right. Of course, you're right." But still I grieved at the loss of this voice that had glorified and praised God.

Recently I was listening to a Jeremy Camp song and thinking, as I have many times before, how much his voice reminds me of the singer who fell away. This wasn't the first time I've had a strong sense that God was saying He had raised up this "voice" in place of the one who had fallen. I decided to do a Google search to see if the facts agreed. I discovered that the year Jeremy Camp gained wide recognition was the same year the former singer left the Christian music scene. God had raised up one of the "seven thousand others who had not bowed the knee to Baal."

While it grieves God's heart when one of his children fall (and I still grieve over the loss of the voice that is gone from the Christian music scene), Scripture tells us if our voices are silent, even the rocks will cry out in praise. (Luke 19:40). God will not leave Himself without a witness to cry out His praise.

Father, how thankful I am that we have your promise
that even if your children prove to be unfaithful to sing your praises,
even the rocks will cry out. Amen.

2018

WHAT DEFINES CHARACTER?
January 11

Some time ago, my friend, Gertrude Slabach, did a blog titled, *The Two Things that Define Character*. She quoted her father as saying, "There are two things that tell the character of a person: settling an estate or building a line fence." Interesting statement.

Immediately, I thought of an example of each of these situations. When we settled my mother's estate, her six children and our spouses gathered in Mother's bedroom. Her will stated that her belongings were to be divided among us, share and share alike, and *no quibbling*!* Someone said Ron, my oldest brother, should choose first since he had been the executor of the will and had done all the work. No arguments there! Ron only wanted one thing, and we all agreed he should have the item he wanted.

As various ones voiced their desires, nearly everyone prefaced their statements with, "If no one else wants this..." and were told promptly, "If you want that, you should have it." Not one objection was raised and there was absolutely "no quibbling." I'm sure there were things more than one person would have liked to have, but on that day, self took a back seat and harmony prevailed. I can't say this has always been true, but in that situation, the Beiler family exhibited good character by Gert's father's standards.

Mother, who loved harmony more than anything, would have been so pleased.

(*Definition of quibbling: arguing or raising objections about a trivial matter.)

The other incident had to do with a line boundary in our neighborhood in Penn Hills that I've already told you about. The character of the person who had bought our house was certainly revealed when she decided to sue our former neighbors whose lane was on a foot or two of her property. It would have caused long-term bitterness and animosity in the neighborhood.

Gertrude's father felt strongly that "a person's true character is shown when it comes to working out differences in our property, our possessions and our money." In these situations, it quickly becomes evident what we value most. For example, in the first incident above, I believe my brothers and sisters had already decided that relationships were more important than possessions. Nothing my mother owned was worth fighting over. In the second example, the woman who bought our house had no relationship with her neighbors and didn't care about them at all. She only gave up the dispute when she thought she herself might be sued by another neighbor.

Make no mistake, our attitudes toward our property, our possessions, and our money matter to God. In Philippians 2:3-4 NIV, the Apostle Paul says, *Do nothing out of selfish ambition or vain conceit, but in humility consider others better than yourselves. Each of you should look not only to your own interests, but also to the interests of others.* If we follow these instructions, it will provide a good foundation for our character, and we will pass the tests of character when they come.

Father, forgive us when we place more value on material things than on relationships. Change our hearts and make us like the One who was "meek and lowly of heart" (Matthew 11:29).

COME TO THE WATER
February 8

Sometimes we get the idea that pastors don't struggle with the same issues we do. We think of them as the ones who help meet *our* needs—not the ones who *have* needs. But this is far from true. I want to share the account of a pastor who is very dear to me and how God met her needs.

My sister, Ruth, sat at home alone one Sunday morning while some one else preached her message at the church where she and her husband were co-pastors. Two weeks earlier, a bad case of flu followed by anxiety attacks had left her so weak she'd needed to sit on a stool to preach. This week their elder chairperson had offered to preach her message because she felt unable to do it. She wondered why God hadn't healed her so she could do what He'd called her to do.

At least when her husband and two children came home from church, she'd be able to hear secondhand how her message had gone. She glanced out the window just in time to see a motorcycle pull into their driveway and recognized the familiar figure of their friend, Paul, a member of their congregation. Paul had the gift of encouragement and she hurried to the door thinking, *Oh good, Paul has come to cheer me up.*

"Then I realized Paul was holding a small, white plastic cup of water. I recognized it at once. The theme of my message had been *Come to the Water.* The cups and water were to be provided so anyone who was thirsty for God could come and get a drink after the sermon.

"Paul greeted me and said, 'All during Sunday School and Church, I couldn't get you off my mind. We had a wonderful message about coming to the water, and afterward, a compelling invitation for those who needed a touch from God to come up for a drink. Almost everyone came to receive God's touch through the symbolic cup of water.'

"Paul studied me with compassionate eyes. 'Then I realized that the person who should have been there preaching that wonderful sermon, the one who needed God's healing touch the most, wasn't there.

So I've brought you a cup of water so you, too, can receive God's touch in your life.'

"With tears streaming down my cheeks, I took the cup of water and drank. I felt as though God's love enveloped me as Paul wrapped his arms around me in a big bear hug. 'No matter how long it takes for you to get well, the church will wait and stand by you because we love you and need you.'

"I knew then that God hadn't forgotten me. In His wisdom, He'd known that, more than I'd needed to *preach* my sermon, I had needed to be a *recipient* of its message. In His mercy, He'd sent Paul as His messenger so that I, too, could *Come to the Water*."

I hope we will be as sensitive as Paul to the needs of our pastors, to be the people who offer them symbolic cups of cold water when they need it most, remembering they are human, too.

Father, thank you for our pastors who serve so faithfully. Help us be
more discerning of times when they need a touch from you
through our willing hands. Amen.

WHAT IS SELFLESSNESS?
February 22

I've been rereading a wonderful book by Cynthia Heald called, *Life Promises for Women* which contains a section on "Selflessness." For the most part, I agree with what Cynthia shares on this subject, but as I read and reread her definition of selflessness, red flags waved. She says, "If I had to write a definition of selflessness, I think it would be this: *willingly sacrificing oneself for the needs of others in order to truly live.*

Her definition sounds so good and quite spiritual, but if taken without any disclaimers, can lead to our downfall. I believe this is especially true for Christian women, me included.

For many years, I was oh so willing to sacrifice myself for the needs of others, and my mercy and compassion gifts attracted needy people like flies. "No" wasn't in my vocabulary and fear of hurting people's feelings often ruled my decisions. Living life this way took me repeatedly to the edge of burn out. As I became more and more overwhelmed by all the needs, I'd come to the point where I didn't even want to go to church because there might be someone there who *needed* me.

When I'd finally had enough, I cried out to God to show me what I was doing wrong. The answer didn't come easily but when I was ready to listen, God's still small voice brought Hebrews 4:10 to mind—*for anyone who enters God's rest also rests from his own work, just as God did from His.*

God had actually brought this verse to my attention a year earlier, but I hadn't processed it well. As I walked through one of the toughest seasons of my life, I learned that even sacrificing myself for others needed to be led by the Holy Spirit.

The day God spoke Hebrews 4:10 to me for the second time, the Holy Spirit began to teach me in a variety of ways how to *enter into the rest of God* and *rest from my own works.* I found a book/workbook called *How to Escape the Messiah Trap* by Carmen Berry and made an appointment with myself every week to process the information. I had to evaluate every relationship to determine whether it was healthy, and begin to focus more on spending time with people with whom I had healthy relationships.

Carmen says, "In a balanced, healthy friendship, both parties take turns talking and listening, leaning and supporting, giving and taking." At that time, I had very few of those relationships. It was hard for me to focus on relationships with people who weren't needy. It felt selfish.

During my struggle, I felt so alone because I didn't know anyone else fighting this battle. In His mercy, God brought me a helper named Marie. As I listened to Marie bring a message, I knew I needed what she had. She told us she began every day affirming, "I choose today by an act of my will to bring my entire spirit, soul, and body under the reign of your Spirit."

Marie never used the words *entering the rest of God* or *resting from her own work* but I knew that's what she was doing. After I listened to her message and told her that I knew it had been just for me, Marie said, "I believe God is saying you are in a place of transition, at a bridge that connects continents. Would you allow me to help prepare you to walk across that bridge?" (She had no idea we were preparing to go to Japan.)

As we talked one day, Marie said, "I'm hearing a lot of expectations. You can't be led by the Holy Spirit if you're ruled by the expectations of other people." God showed me that my own self-expectations, the expectations of others, and even what I thought others expected of me had kept me from entering His rest. This had resulted in me doing many things that weren't His plan, becoming more involved in situations than was wise, and living without margins. I knew I needed to change.

As I left that session, I "heard" in my spirit the chorus of a worship song, "I will lay down my idols, thrones I have made, all that has taken my heart. Lord, I will bow to you, to no other God but you alone." I wept as I realized all the idols I had served by allowing myself to be ruled by expectations rather than led by the Holy Spirit.

I wish I could say that since then I have always and only been led by the Holy Spirit in every situation, but pleasing people is still my default setting, especially when I find myself in new situations, surrounded by new people. But I'm learning that sometimes true selflessness is being willing to let others think ill of me when I say no to doing things God isn't asking me to do. True selflessness, I've realized, can only be defined by the Holy Spirit.

Father, help us not to assume that being selfless means living lives without boundaries or margins but to understand that true selflessness always includes allowing the Holy Spirit to choose when to sacrifice ourselves for the needs of others. Amen.

DIARY OF A SLOW STARTER
March 22

Most of us have experienced times when things came easily to others but were difficult for us—maybe in school our classmates were solving for X when we were still trying to figure out why anyone cared! (I still don't know why anyone cares!) Maybe all our friends had their licenses and we still found ourselves petrified at the thought of getting behind the wheel. Or maybe as young parents, our friends were enjoying their infants while our babies squalled all day and all night.

Whatever the reason, how do we deal with the feeling of being a failure while others succeed? How do we find the courage to try one more time? I want to share our daughter, Angelyn's, story. (Diary of a Slow Starter as told to Daisy Townsend.)

May 15, 1989 – Today I celebrated my sixteenth birthday. Most of my friends are excited about learning to drive, but the stick shift on our VW Golf scares me silly. I don't know if I'll even bother to get my permit.

May 22, 1989 – My friends talked me into getting my permit. Passing the permit test was easy compared to trying to coax our little, almost-yellow car into the next gear. To make matters worse, Robbie already has his license. How can we be twins and be so different? He's driving to Dairy Queen and the mall while I'm still stalling in the driveway.

September 18, 1989 – I know I'll never be able to drive this car, but we renewed my permit today in case I get brave.

January 15, 1990 – This is getting embarrassing. I'm so sick of explaining why I don't have my license and depending on other people to take me where I want to go. I keep renewing my permit even though I know there's no way I'm going to drive this car in the snow.

May 21, 1990 – I have hope. We got a second car with an automatic shift. At last I'll be able to drive. No more depending on my family and friends to run simple errands for me. I can be independent just as soon as I get that little piece of paper in my hand. I'm between permits right now (waiting for my fourth one), but it should be here soon.

May 31, 1990 – My permit came a couple days ago, and I've been driving everywhere—making up for lost time. I've almost got Dad and Mom convinced I'm ready to take my test.

June 4, 1990 – I took my driver's test today. I was a nervous wreck. I guess God knew I wasn't ready to be a licensed driver yet. I begged Him to help me pass, but I failed. How will I ever find the courage to try again? Maybe I'll be asking people to drive me around for the rest of my life.

September 24, 1990 – Tomorrow is the last day I can take my test on this permit. I wanted to make sure I was ready this time. If I fail, I'll have to retake the permit test since this is my fourth permit. I'm so scared. I probably won't sleep a wink tonight.

September 25, 1990 A.M. Last night when I couldn't sleep, I started to pray. Philippians 4:13 came to my mind, "I can do all things through Christ which strengthens me." I knew that verse was from God and that all my fear was from Satan. I *can* pass my driver's test. With the words of that verse running through my mind, I finally fell asleep.

This morning I felt much calmer, but I looked up another reference on fear for good measure. "Because the Lord is at my right hand, I will not be shaken" (Psalm 16:8). Wow! God is going to sit at my right hand today while I take this test. What more could I want? I'm not 100 percent calm, but I'm not nearly as nervous as I was the last time.

September 25, 1990 P.M. – All the way to the police station, I kept repeating, "I can do all things through Christ… I can do all things through Christ…" At the barracks when Office Peters got in beside me, I whispered, "The Lord is at my right hand…" I whizzed through the course like a pro. This time I *knew* I'd passed. When the officer said,

"Park it next to the curb, Angi," I confidently pulled up to the curb.

"Park it *completely*," he said sternly. I put the car in "park."

"*Completely*, Angi."

My confidence was fading fast. *What did the man want?* I turned the car off, but the officer was still looking at me expectantly. "The Lord is at my right hand." I prayed frantically, "God, what does he want me to do?"

Then I saw it: the emergency brake. I'd never used it in my life, but I yanked on it hard. Almost holding my breath, I forced myself to look at Officer Peters. He nodded, and I breathed again. I had passed! "Take your permit in, and the officer at the desk will stamp it for you," Those were the most beautiful words I'd ever heard.

I wanted to shout, but instead I whispered, "Thanks, Lord, for being at my right hand. I *can* do all things through You."

What things in your life leave you feeling defeated and unable to find the courage to try one more time? Anne Graham Lotz says,

What problem are you facing that's bigger than you? ...Focus on who God is—then look at your problems. He puts things into proper perspective. Because there's nothing you face—not a big debt, or big job, or big fear that's bigger than He is or beyond His power to change!

Father, whatever problem we face, help us remember that because you are at our right hand, we will not be shaken, and we can do all things through Christ which strengthens us. Amen.

SMEARS AND SMUCGES
April 4

Recently an acquaintance invited me to view a slide show of flowers on her I-Pad. I was delighted until I saw her screen—so smeared with fingerprints and smudges that I couldn't concentrate on the magnificent flowers. The woman didn't apologize or even seem to notice the condition of her screen. She probably didn't even see the smears because she was used to them.

Over the next few days, the Holy Spirit brought this event to mind again and again, as He often does when He wants me to look for a spiritual truth in a secular situation. Could it be, I wondered, that people are distracted from seeing the beauty of Jesus in us because our lives are smeared with sin and character flaws that have been part of us for so long we don't see them or notice how offensive they are?

Throughout the seasons of my life, the Holy Spirit has taken me and others I love through many times of cleansing and pruning to remove the smears and smudges. Step one was making me aware of the sin or character flaw. Here's a portion of one devotional from my book, Homespun Faith, *The Giant Makeover*, telling how God prepared us for going as missionaries to Japan:

"God continues to place me in situations exquisitely orchestrated to bring to the surface weaknesses that have been well hidden. Sometimes only I am aware of how badly I'm reacting inwardly, and sometimes it becomes apparent to those around me. Anger and embarrassment usually rise in me and, eventually, a feeling of helplessness to change the deeply ingrained pattern."

None of us like to feel helpless. None of us like to feel embarrassed by our weaknesses. None of us like to feel that we're caught in a pattern we don't know how to break. But here's what I discovered:

"Uncomfortable as it is, the feeling of helplessness is necessary for the correction process. Each of us must realize that we are not able to change our behavior or our attitudes except by God's grace as we repent and cooperate with Him." (Homespun Faith)

There's a reason the Twelve Step Program begins with admitting we are powerless over our problem but believe that a power greater than ourselves can restore us to sanity. Then comes making a searching and fearless moral inventory of ourselves, admitting to God, ourselves and another human being the exact nature of our wrongs, and finally, becoming entirely ready to have God remove all these defects of character.

The fancy word for this process in the lives of Christians is sanctification, the process by which we become more and more like Jesus. Positionally, we are new creatures in Christ from the moment of salvation, but practically, Christians are all in a process of transformation.

After sharing many examples of the sanctification process in Homespun Faith, I discovered it's not always a popular subject. One review implied that I *spent too much time polishing the window rather than just enjoying the view*. At the same time, they added that I was "*a lovely person who lights up the space around her.*" I smiled because if I "light up the space around me," it's because Jesus has *polished my windows* to remove many of the smears and smudges that kept His light from shining through me.

Those whom I [dearly and tenderly] love, I tell their faults and convict and convince and reprove and chasten [I discipline and instruct them](Revelation 3:19 AMP). *God disciplines us for our good that we may share in His holiness (*Hebrews 12:10 NIV).

God loves me just the way I am today, but much too much to let me stay that way (author unknown) is an important truth to remember as we allow the transformation process to continue. My hope is to let the Holy Spirit continue to conform me to the image of Christ so that my "caterpillar days" would be just a distant memory to me and those who knew me then.

Thank you, Father, for loving me enough to tell me what I don't want to hear and being patient during the transformation process. Amen.

A NEW DISCIPLINE
April 19

My mother used to say, "I've never known anyone who loves to argue as much as the Beilers" (my maiden name). She was right! For example, my grandfather, John Beiler, was never wrong, and I learned it was useless to argue with him. In the next generation, I can still see the look on my father's face when he strongly disagreed with something my mother said. I can still hear the tone of his voice when he adamantly said, "NO!" She rarely bothered to argue with *him* either.

Although in some settings with some people, I tend to keep my opinions to myself, in others, my default setting is to argue. I can hardly bear to stop until the other person admits they're wrong.

Recently Donn and I read a devotional about a college professor who didn't argue with a student who had made some pretty strong comments in class about the professor and his philosophies. The professor just thanked the student for sharing his opinion and went on with the class.

Afterward, when asked why he had not rebutted, the professor said, "I'm practicing my new discipline of not needing to have the last word." Wow! What a novel idea! Would it be possible for a Beiler to practice that discipline?

Not long after that, another devotional spoke to me. The author, Pamela Dorrel, says, "It has always been easy for me to get into debates with friends and family, and I find myself arguing more than I should. If I make others angry, I regret it, and I'm always willing to apologize and move on. I just can't pass up a rousing exchange of ideas about current events."

Then one day in the middle of a debate with her father that had turned into an argument, Pamela suddenly forgot what she was going to say! The only thing she could remember was this verse: "I treasure your word in my heart, so that I may not sin against you" (Psalm 119:11). Pamela says, "In an instant, my perspective changed. I realized I was so caught up in the conversation that I was about to say something hurtful to my father just to 'win' the argument. I held my tongue that day, and we called a truce."

I wondered how often I had said something hurtful just to win the argument. In the heat of the moment, it's so easy to do

Years ago after a discussion on the tongue at a prayer group I attended, I remember praying aloud that God would put a guard on our mouths (Psalm 141 NIV). One of the women who loved arguing and being right at least as much as I did laughed out loud. She apologized but said she'd been picturing the size guard it would take to keep her mouth shut!

Ecclesiastes 3:7 says there is a time to speak and a time to be silent. During a family vacation when our kids were teenagers, Donn had finally had enough of me arguing with our son in the car. My normally mild-mannered husband said, *"Don't argue with him. He knows!"* That was a hard pill for me to swallow because it strongly interfered with me having the last word, but Donn was right. Whatever might be coming out of our son's mouth, he had heard the truth enough times that we didn't need to argue with him. It was time to be quiet.

Years later our son was sharing a situation where it was so hard for him to stop arguing, even though he knew it would do no good. I laughed and read to him the scripture I'd adapted and prayed for him that morning, even though I wasn't aware of this particular struggle. "May he not have anything to do with foolish and stupid arguments, because they produce quarrels, and may he recognize that the Lord's servant must not quarrel; instead he must be kind to everyone, able to teach, not resentful." (from II Timothy 2)

I'm asking the Holy Spirit to prompt me when it's time to practice the new discipline I'm learning. I'm finding that when I'm tuned in to the Holy Spirit and surrendered to Him, even a Beiler can choose not to have the last word.

Forgive us, Father, when self and pride lure us into arguments. Thank you that by your grace, we're never too old to change. Amen

By FAITH OR BY SIGHT?
June 7

The very essence of homespun faith is learning from the object lessons God gives us in nature and in the every-day happenings of our lives. If we have eyes to see and ears to hear, the Holy Spirit can teach us many things.

Recently God has been using the dahlia bulbs we planted earlier this spring to teach us a lesson about faith. A week or two after we planted the bulbs, we started worrying because we saw no signs of growth. Every day one of us checked the flower bed. Finally, I Googled to find out how long it should take for dahlias to sprout.

I didn't find much that was helpful since we couldn't remember when we'd planted them. However, someone did suggest that one could dig (gently) in the area where the rhizome was planted to see if there was any sign of life. After a significant amount of digging, Donn found a tiny bit of growth that MIGHT be a dahlia. But was it really a dahlia? And even if it was, how did we know it wasn't the only one that had sprouted?

A few days later, Donn picked up four potted dahlias that were already blooming at Kraynak's. We planted them in larger pots and were prepared to transplant them into our flower bed if the dahlias didn't grow. The next day Donn spotted our first, for-sure dahlia above ground. We were excited, but still hesitant to believe others would follow. In spite of our negativity, almost every day, Donn showed me another sprout that had broken through the soil.

Last night as we counted our dahlias, Donn said, "There are only two that didn't come up."

I said, "Yet!"

Shaking his head, Donn responded, "Oh we of little faith!"

I laughed because I had already been planning this blog about how God was showing us how much our faith depends on sight. No matter how many dahlias sprouted, we still didn't believe the others would come up until we SAW the green leaves above ground. In much the same way, we often pray for something but don't really believe God will answer until we see the results--or perhaps even then, we find some other explanations than God answering our prayer.

I'm reminded of the early church who prayed earnestly for Peter when Herod put him in prison. Surely they were praying for his release, but listen to their response when Rhoda came to tell them he was at the door. *"You're out of your mind," they told her (*Acts 12:15 NIV*).*

This object lesson on faith has had me examining my attitude when I pray. Am I praying expectantly or am I just saying words with no real belief that my prayers will be answered? Would I be as surprised as the early church if God answered my prayer? Far too often recently, I've thought or even said, "God are you even listening when I pray? Do the prayers I pray make any difference or am I wasting my time?"

Last week someone dear to us for whom I've been praying every day for many years asked if he could talk to us. As we sat on the porch swing, he said, "I've finally realized I can't make it without God in my life." We've passed his house several times since to find him in his back yard reading his Bible, he's like a sponge soaking up God's Word. We're encouraged and rejoicing in this answer to prayer.

And yet Hebrews 11:1 tells us *Now faith is being **sure** of what we **hope for** and **certain of what we do not see**.* And II Corinthians 5:7 says, *We walk by faith and not by sight.* In light of what God is teaching us and the truth of these Scriptures, I'm asking Him to help me see the people for whom I pray through eyes of faith. I'm asking Him to keep my faith strong even when it appears my prayers are in vain. I'm asking Him to enable me to believe He IS working in their lives even when I SEE no evidence of it. I don't want to be surprised when He answers my prayers!

Amazing, Almighty Heavenly Father, thank you for all the incredible ways you answer prayer. Help us not to be were *slow of heart to believe* (Luke 24:25). Increase our expectancy and our belief in your willingness to answer our prayers. Amen.

Spiritual Blindness
June 14

When our daughter, Angi, and I went out to lunch recently, we talked about our frustrations when dealing with people who are spiritually blind. It reminded me of an incident many years ago when one of my relatives had started making impassioned accusations that simply were not based in reality.

I kept saying to myself afterward, *She's so blind! She's so blind!* In my bewilderment, God made it clear that her perceptions were distorted because she was spiritually blind in this situation. Her vision had been affected, perhaps by hidden wounds or unforgiveness, and had produced inappropriate behavior.

That night Donn and I stayed in the home of a friend we don't visit often. There were no nightlights, and when I got up to go to the bathroom in the middle of the night, I became completely disoriented. As I stood, trying to get my bearings in the complete darkness of the unfamiliar hall, I remembered the incident that day with my loved one. Struggling to find my way back to our room in the smothering darkness, my irritation with her turned to compassion.

As Angi and I talked about this incident, I also remembered an illustration from one of Eugenia Price's nonfiction books. I don't remember her exact words, but in essence she said, *We don't slap blind people around because they can't see.* Our daughter burst out laughing at the absurdity of that statement, and yet, how often do we judge or verbally beat up people who are spiritually blind?

If this kind of attitude is inappropriate, what should our response be to people we believe are blind spiritually? Since Jesus said He came to give recovery of sight to the blind (Luke 4:18, Isaiah 61:1), I think we should begin by asking Him to restore the spiritually blind person's sight. I believe Jesus wants to bring recovery of sight to the *spiritually* blind just as much as to the *physically* blind—maybe even more.

It's also appropriate to pray for wisdom about the root cause of their spiritual blindness. Just as some people are physically blind from birth, some people are spiritually blind practically from birth because of the way they were raised. Generational strongholds may have been passed down from the parents or grandparents. At other times, spiritual blindness may be brought on by pride, fear, or idolizing a respected person who is spiritually blind in this area.

Whatever the cause, the Holy Spirit is able to reveal it to us as we pray so that we can do battle with the forces of darkness. Ephesians 6:12 KJV says, *We wrestle not against flesh and blood, but against principalities, powers, and spiritual wickedness in high places*, while II Corinthians 10:4 KJV tells us, *The weapons of our warfare are not carnal but mighty through the power of God to the bringing down of strongholds*.

It's no wonder we are so often soundly defeated when we try to fight spiritual battles in the natural with carnal weapons. When I become angry with people who, in light of Scripture, are clearly spiritually blind, I try to remember Eugenia Price's statement and ask God to change my attitude to one of compassionate love.

Lord Jesus, only you can bring recovery of sight
to the spiritually blind by the power of your Holy Spirit. Forgive us
when we respond in unloving ways. Give us clear vision so we can join
you in the battle to restore sight to those who cannot see. Amen.

Visually Impaired by our Culture?
June 27

When we went to Japan, it didn't take long to notice that public displays of affection, such as holding hands, weren't common, especially among the older generation. One Sunday when people had brought pictures of those who had passed away to honor them, I noticed a picture of an elderly husband and wife holding hands.

"Oh look," I said to the pastor's wife, "they're holding hands!"

She smiled and responded, "She's blind."

Although Donn and I still laugh when we think about this incident and are prone to say, "She's probably blind," when we see unlikely couples holding hands, it made me wonder how often we make wrong assumptions about people who haven't been raised in the same culture we have.

In Japan it's sometimes considered rude to walk or stand while eating, so sometimes foreigners who do this might be considered rude. Our plea at times in various situations was that we weren't rude—just ignorant! On the other hand, there may have been times that we deemed the Japanese people to be rude when they were just acting in ways that were culturally acceptable in their country.

Years ago I submitted an article to a publication in Canada with a self-addressed, stamped envelope for their response. When I didn't hear from them within a reasonable amount of time, I contacted the editor. I received a vehement answer saying I probably hadn't heard from them because we "arrogant Americans" assumed the whole world used OUR postage. Rather than assuming I'd made a mistake or didn't know, it fit this editor's bias toward Americans to believe I was arrogant.

Lately I've been aware that we may also misunderstand others who haven't been raised in the same spiritual culture we have. Some time ago, a lady sitting behind me at church leaned forward to whisper to me about the young man behind us who was so rude and disrespectful he hadn't removed his hat when he came into the church. She dismissed my suggestion that perhaps he had never been taught that a man should remove his hat in church. I suspect that her bias toward the younger generation is that they are rude.

Some people are also offended because churches with coffee shops have put seats with cup holders in their sanctuaries, believing that people who bring coffee into the sanctuary are being disrespectful. Others believe those who dress casually to attend church are showing disrespect. Years ago a woman in the church we attended hated the songbooks with bright yellow flowers on the front cover, perhaps thinking such gaudy covers didn't show proper reverence. I suspect these differences of opinion, these biases, among different cultures— spiritual and physical--have much more to do with how we were raised than with right and wrong.

So how can we live in harmony with those who think differently than we do about these issues? Two scriptures come to mind: "Love always believes the best" (I Corinthians 13:7), and "Let love be your greatest aim" (I Corinthians 14:1). I believe we could avoid many misunderstandings if we chose to believe the best of those with whom we disagree, instead of believing the worst, and if we allowed love, rather than being right, to be our highest goal. I believe cultural biases can be overcome when we choose to see each other through eyes of love.

Father, forgive us for being so quick to believe the worst. Help us believe the best and let love be our greatest aim. Amen.

FOG WARNING
July 12

The sun was shining as I pulled into a parking lot at Presque Isle. When I opened my IPad to check the weather, a dense fog alert appeared. I smiled. The warning was a bit late for me.

The dense fog had surprised me about an hour earlier. I slowed down and turned on my lights. Braver (or more foolish) drivers, unconcerned by limited visibility, whizzed around me. When I pulled into a familiar rest stop, I became so disoriented that I crept back to the Interstate, breathing a sigh of relief when I was on the road again.

I decided not to stop at the Walmart along Route 79 as I'd planned. I had no idea which exit to use because the store was usually visible from the Interstate. After my experience at the rest stop, I was concerned that if I did manage to find the store, I'd never find my way back to the road.

In this case, the fact that the warning came too late didn't affect the outcome of my trip, except to delay my arrival. However, this isn't always the case. A warning for an earthquake, tsunami, or nuclear attack that comes too late can have catastrophic consequences—as can denialist propaganda by companies minimizing or negating the dangers of the products they produce. (Even though it was known as early as the 1940's and 1950's that smoking cigarettes caused lung cancer, many people—even doctors—didn't believe it.)

Sometimes the issue isn't that the warning is too late—the issue is the way we respond to the warning. After I arrived in Erie the day of the heavy fog, I talked to a woman about the redwing blackbirds I was observing through my binoculars. She told me she'd heard those birds can become aggressive when nesting. I was raised in the country and had never experienced an aggressive redwing blackbird, so I discounted her warning.

The next day I saw a sign along the bike path: "Redwing blackbirds become aggressive when nesting. They are nesting in this area." I was surprised but told myself that as long as I remained on the path I would be safe. I didn't even worry when a redwing blackbird hovered over the path above my head, scolding loudly. Then in a flash, the bird dive bombed my hair as I screamed and ran!

After I calmed down, I began warning the people approaching the area where I'd been attacked. I could tell by their response whether they'd ever been attacked by blackbirds. Those who hadn't were just as unconcerned as I had been. Those who had, appreciated the warning and took it seriously.

Later, when I walked back the way I'd come, I couldn't remember exactly where I'd encountered the vicious blackbird. I was thankful when a lady said, "Watch out for those redwing blackbirds! They just got me again!" I left the path and walked as close to the road as I could. My response to the warning changed because I knew the danger was real.

Thankfully, God's warnings never come too late. However, the way we respond to His warnings can mean the difference between spiritual or even physical death. Deuteronomy 30:19 says: *This day I call the heavens and the earth as witnesses against you that I have set before you life and death, blessings and curses. Now choose life, so that you and your children may live.* In my next devotional I want to talk more about the warnings God gives and ways we respond.

Father, warnings are only beneficial
when we believe there is danger. Help us not to change the
meaning of your warnings or buy into denialist propaganda of our
culture that would cause us to negate them. Amen.

FOG WARNING
Part II
July 18

In my previous devotional I talked about the fog warning that came too late when I went to Presque Isle, as well as the aggressive redwing blackbird warning I discounted. I said sometimes the issue isn't that the warning is too late—the issue is the way we respond to the warning.

The same is certainly true of the warnings we receive from God. While Noah heeded God's warning of the coming flood and built an ark, there's no record of anyone except Noah's family making any effort to board the ark. Although the Bible doesn't mention the details, I'm sure people must have asked Noah why he was building this gargantuan boat, and he must have warned them of the coming flood. However, no one else prepared for the disaster.

In the account of Sodom and Gomorrah, even Lot and his family, who received a personal warning, were not in any hurry to leave the city. When Lot warned his sons-in-law, they thought he was joking, and Lot himself and his family only left when the men (probably angels) grasped their hands and led them out.

The reactions of the people in these two accounts, as well as those I mentioned previously, lead me to believe warnings are not particularly effective in getting most people to change their behavior unless something bad has already happened to convince them the warnings are valid. Both the people in Noah's day and those who were warned in Sodom and Gomorrah discounted the warnings because they didn't believe the danger was real.

However, the response of Noah was different. Although Noah had never experienced a flood—it had never even rained before, he didn't hesitate to heed God's warning. Why was his reaction different? Verse 9 of Chapter six of Genesis says: *Noah was a righteous man, blameless among the people of his time, and he walked with God.*

. Noah trusted God and was obedient even when the people in his culture very likely laughed at him for being so foolish as to build an ark. He didn't allow anything to sway him from heeding God's warning. I believe the difference in Noah's reaction is found in his relationship with God.

In the account of Sodom and Gomorrah, we find that the first personal warning from God was actually given to Abraham, Lot's uncle, not to Lot. Verse seventeen of Genesis eighteen says, *"The Lord said, 'Shall I hide from Abraham what I am about to do?"* Because of Abraham's close relationship with God, He would not destroy the city where Abraham's nephew lived without telling him.

Abraham believed the warning God gave and interceded for Sodom and Gomorrah, begging God to spare the cities if even as few as ten righteous people could be found. When even ten were not found, God was still faithful to Abraham by sending urgent messengers to his beloved nephew and his family.

What about us? How do we respond to God's warnings because of the depth of our relationship with Him? If warnings were only being given to those who are "righteous, blameless among the people of our time, and who walk with God," would we qualify? Do we heed God's warnings regardless of the mocking of our culture? God help us to rise up and be the Noahs and the Abrahams of our day.

Father, may we be righteous people, blameless among the people of our time, whose relationship with you is our top priority. Give us ears to hear the voice of your Spirit and hearts that choose to walk with you, even if it means being out of step with our culture. Amen.

WARNINGS FROM THE GOSPELS
July 26

In my last couple devotionals, we've been talking about different kinds of warnings and our responses to them. I've said my experience has led me to believe warnings are not particularly effective in getting most people to change their behavior unless something bad has already happened to convince them the warnings are valid. The exception we found in the Old Testament is that people with a deep relationship with God were more apt to heed His warnings, regardless of their culture.

Now I want to look at some New Testament warnings--some in the Gospels and some in the Epistles.

In Matthew 3, we find John the Baptist warning people to repent and be baptized. When the Pharisees and the Sadducees came to where he was baptizing, he chastised them with strong words, including "Produce fruit in keeping with repentance." In other words, being baptized without repentance has no value.

When someone dear to me was preparing to go away to college, he was told by his pastor that he needed to be baptized. He was never asked the vital question about whether he had surrendered his life to Jesus Christ and repented of his sins, which he had not. Those who are considering baptism should make sure they've received Jesus and produced fruit in keeping with repentance.

In Matthew 16, Jesus gave a warning to his disciples: *Be on your guard against the yeast of the Pharisees and Sadducees.* Later, He explained this meant to be on guard against their teachings. I believe this is still valid today as a warning against legalism. I know of a situation where a man became so embroiled in legalism that he no longer believed his father, a wonderful, godly man, was saved because he didn't worship on Saturday. Legalism is truly like yeast because it grows and spreads. Years ago I read about a group who kept adding more and more laws and rules to their Christianity until finally the leaders themselves weren't able to keep them all.

Sound familiar? Jesus said, *The teachers of the religious law and the Pharisees are the official interpreters of the law of Moses. So practice and obey whatever they tell you, but don't follow their example. For they don't practice what they teach. They crush people with unbearable religious demands and never lift a finger to ease the burden* (Matthew 23:2-4 NLT). Sometimes the most sincere people, the ones who most want to please Jesus, can be the most susceptible to legalism, thinking that they are pleasing God.

Here are a few of the other warnings of Jesus:

Watch out! Be on your guard against wanting to have more and more things. Life is not made up of how much a person has (Luke 12:15 NIRV).

Be careful that you don't do your charitable giving before men, to be seen by them, or else you have no reward with your Father who is in heaven (Matthew 6:1 WEB).

Be careful therefore how you hear... My mother and my brothers are these who hear the word of God, and do it (Luke 8:18, 21 WEB).

Lord Jesus, thank you for loving us enough to warn us of the things that will lead us away from you and make you sad. Give us ears to hear the voice of your Spirit and hearts to obey. Amen.

WARNINGS FROM THE EPISTLES
July 31

"Truth is truth even if no one believes it and a lie is a lie even if everyone believes it." (author unknown)

Our journey through warnings now takes us to warnings in the Epistles. We'll start with I John 4:1 NIV. *Dear friends, do not believe every spirit, but test the spirits to see whether they are from God, because many false prophets have gone out into the world.* I don't believe we've ever lived in a day when this warning was needed more because deception is rampant on so many fronts, whether the spirits are tempting people to legalism or to political correctness and liberal theology.

Sadly these spirits spread their deceptions in universities and seminaries where our young people and future ministers are being trained. Someone dear to me was sometimes deceived because he was impressed by people with more education than he had. Having a lot of letters after one's name does not insure that a person is wise and well-trained in the things of God. Remember Simeon in Luke 2, described only as "righteous and devout," who immediately recognized Jesus as the Messiah, while the Pharisees and the teachers of the law plotted to kill Him.

The last warning from the Epistles I want to touch on is I Peter 5:8 NIV. *Be self-controlled and alert. Your enemy the devil prowls around like a roaring lion looking for someone to devour.* Again, I think we've never lived in a time when we need this warning more than we need it now. I believe Satan knows his time is short, and he's working harder than ever. As I mentioned before, I think one of his shiniest weapons is deception. I read once that if we love anyone or anything more than we love the truth, we will be deceived. I agree.

Truth sounds like hate to those who hate the truth. (Author unknown)

Our main weapon against Satan and deception is the truth. It's included in Ephesians six in the full armor of God as "the belt of truth." I'm told that in Roman armor, the belt held together the armor above and below the waist, so if the belt was missing, the other armor would not stay in place. I believe the same is true of the armor of God—if the belt of truth is missing, the other pieces of armor will not be effective.

In II Corinthians 10:4 NIV, we're told, *The weapons we fight with are not the weapons of the world. On the contrary, they have divine power to demolish strongholds. We demolish arguments and every pretension that sets itself up against the knowledge of God, and we take captive every thought to make it obedient to Christ.* Here again, truth is the most powerful weapon we have to demolish strongholds, arguments and every pretension that sets itself up against the knowledge of God. It is what helps us take captive every thought in obedience to Christ.

In the days in which we live, how desperately we need to be warned about Satan's attacks and how desperately we need to pray for God's truth to be our foundation.

Father, thank you for the warnings that fill your Word. Give us ears to hear the voice of your Spirit to properly apply the Word of Truth. Shield us from deception regardless of how educated the deceiver may be.
Amen.

WARNINGS FROM WATCHMEN
August 9

We've been talking about warnings for some time—warnings in general and warnings from God—as well as our response to them. So what about the day in which we live? Does God still give warnings and do we have a role to play in the warnings being given?

Let's look at God's Word to Ezekiel in Ezekiel 3:17-19NIV.

Son of man, I have made you a watchman for the house of Israel; so hear the word I speak and give them warning from me. When I say to a wicked man, 'You will surely die,' and you do not warn him or speak out to dissuade him from his evil ways in order to save his life, that wicked man will die for his sin, and I will hold you accountable for his blood. But if you do warn the wicked man and he does not turn from his wickedness or from his evil ways, he will die for his sin; but you will have saved yourself.

Darris McNeely says, "Notice it is *God's* message, not Ezekiel's message or any other prophet's message. It is always God's message delivered *through* the human instrument. The warning comes from God in language phrased to fit the situation and designed to bring people to repentance."

I love the purpose given for the warning in the passage in Ezekiel: "in order to save [the wicked man's] life." So the purpose for giving someone a warning from God is to save their lives, or as Darris McNeely says, the warnings are designed to bring people to repentance.

I also love the fact that the person delivering the message is not responsible for whether or not the person repents. His/her only responsibility is to deliver the message.

In the New Testament we're told in Galatians:

Brothers, if someone is caught in a sin, you who are spiritual should restore him gently. But watch yourself, or you also may be tempted (Galatians 6:1 NIV).

As this passage indicates, the attitude of the person delivering the warning, as well as the purpose, is of utmost importance.

There's no doubt in my mind that God still gives warnings and that sometimes He gives them through "watchmen" in the body of Christ. However, many of us are so worried about sounding negative or judgmental or politically incorrect, that few of us are bold enough to be His messengers. I quake when I read Ezekiel 3:18 which says if we do not pass along his warning, God will hold us accountable.

I've found myself in the position of being God's messenger more than once and it's without a doubt my least favorite role in the body of Christ. I don't deliver warnings or messages unless I'm so sure that for me *not* to do it would be disobedience.

At times God shows me things so I can pray for someone; at other times, I have to speak. Knowing the difference requires great discernment. Sometimes I seek guidance and direction for weeks or even months before I know what to do. If we're sure God has given us a warning to deliver, we have to decide whether to be ruled by an unhealthy fear of man or a healthy fear of God.

I love The Message's rendering of Matthew 10:28. *Don't be bluffed into silence by the threats of bullies. There's nothing they can do to your soul, your core being. Save your fear for God, who holds your entire life—body and soul—in his hands.* Will unhealthy fear of man prevent us from delivering God's message or will a healthy fear of God prompt us to obey?

Father, if you give us a warning to deliver to someone who is "caught in a sin," give us the courage to be obedient. Enable us to choose not to be ruled by fear of man but by a healthy fear of you. Amen.

I HAVE A DISASTER PLANNED FOR YOU
August 15

"God was speaking to Israel through Jeremiah, saying, 'Unless you change the way you're living, I have a disaster planned for you.'"

Our son's teen years were stormy, and there were times when the Holy Spirit required me to be the "Watchman" to whom He gave warnings for him. This particular day our pastor was preaching from the book of Jeremiah, and I had the strong sense that God was speaking to our son who sat beside me in the sanctuary.. But was he even listening?

The next day, I sat alone in our living room, Bible on my lap. "Lord, were you speaking to Robb yesterday?" I closed my Bible. "I don't think he was listening, and I'm not going to tell him unless you make it very clear that I should."

Robb often didn't respond well to my efforts to speak truth into his life. I no longer did that without a clearly opened door from God.

The outer door to our house opened, and Robb walked in. Why hadn't I heard the car?

"Hello there," I greeted as he came into the living room and plopped down in a chair across from me.

He stared at me. "Well?"

"Well what?" I responded.

"Well, what are you thinking about?"

I groaned inwardly. I had promised God to speak if He clearly opened the door. I met Robb's unwavering gaze. "Were you listening to the pastor's message yesterday?"

He shrugged. "No."

I bit my lip. "Pastor Rich said God told Jeremiah that unless Israel changed the way they were living, He had a disaster planned for them."

Robb was silent.

"So, I don't know what's going on in your life, but I believe that's what God is saying to you. If you don't change the way you're living, He has a disaster planned for you."

Still Robb said nothing. He didn't deny that God might be saying

He had a disaster planned for him, but neither did He acknowledge it. When I remained silent, he finally got to his feet and left the room. I didn't mention our conversation again and neither did he. I had done my part, the rest was up to the Holy Spirit.

A day or two later, our insurance company called. Robb had had three car accidents in the past year, two of which had been his fault. Erie Insurance was informing us that if he was cited in the most recent one, we would be given a surcharged rate, much higher than our present one. Our only other option was to remove him as a driver from our policy.

When Donn came home from work, I told him about the phone call. We both agreed if Robb was cited, we would have no choice but to remove Robb as an insured driver. We simply couldn't afford to pay the surcharge rate.

I knew that for our teen-age son, who loved the freedom that came with driving, losing the ability to drive our car would be a disaster. Was this the disaster God had promised if Robb didn't change his ways?

Once again, I don't remember that Robb argued or tried to change our minds when we told him of this development. Days turned into weeks, and even months went by. I sensed that God was using this time of uncertainty to do a work in Robb's heart.

At last one day the phone call we'd been waiting for came. The insurance companies had decided that no one would be cited in this accident, since it appeared that each person had some share of the blame. If my memory serves me, the damage to our car was so slight that we either didn't have it fixed or didn't turn it in to insurance. There would be no surcharge on our policy.

We never did discover what was going on in our son's life—only he and God knew. But how merciful for God to give Robb a warning so that the disaster planned for him could be averted.

When we receive a warning, we always have a choice—to change our ways or to continue on the path that leads to disaster. Here is the account of one of Israel's interactions with God after the initial warning in chapter 4 of Jeremiah:

This is what the Lord says: "Stand at the crossroads and look; ask for the ancient paths, ask where the good way is, and walk in it, and you will find rest for your souls." But you said, "We will not walk in it."

I appointed watchmen over you and said, "Listen to the sound of the trumpet!" But you said, "We will not listen."

Therefore hear, O nations; observe, O witnesses, what will happen to them. Hear, O earth: I am bringing disaster on the people, the fruit of their schemes, because they have not listened to my words and have rejected my law. (Jeremiah 6:16-19)

Sadly, Israel ignored God's warning, and the disaster that could have been avoided came. Only you can determine how your story will end.

Father, soften our hearts so that we will heed our warnings and repent before it is too late. Amen.

MEMORIES
August 23

On the evening of August 15, we were shocked to learn that my oldest sister, Lulie,* was lying unresponsive in a hospital in Chattanooga, Tennessee, near where she lived. She passed away Monday morning, August 20, just hours after the father of her children, Bud,* went into the presence of the Lord in a hospital in Oakland, Maryland.

I've been sorting through my memories ever since the phone call, traveling to Tennessee and spending time at the hospital with other members of our family.

The process reminds me of a jeweler sorting through precious stones, turning them in various directions to see what they look like when they catch the light. Some of my memories sparkle and bring me joy, while others are dark and bring me to tears. Some I can share while others are too personal to bring into public view.

Lulie was almost exactly nine years older than I am, both of us born in June. I'm sure I caused her

(*Lucy and Mark were their given names, but we never called them anything but Lulie and Bud for reasons unknown to me.)

146

endless frustration as little sisters do, but I know she loved me dearly and her two other younger sisters. It couldn't have been easy for her to share a bedroom with the "girlies," because of the age difference. She and I shared one double bed, while Judy and Ruthie shared another.

My memories of those days include Lulie reading to us after the four of us were in bed. She read books we loved like *Nancy and Plum*, which was filled with *Nancy said, Plum said, Nancy said, Plum said*, which must have been a trial to her writer's sensibilities, and *Prairie School,* which was literally falling apart from the many times it had been read.

Before we went to sleep, I also remember her writing in her diary with her favorite fountain pen, Druscilla, which often left green ink stains on her middle finger. She would tuck her diary under the mattress to hide it, perhaps from our big brother Ron? Certainly her little sisters knew where it was. I don't remember ever reading it, but I'd be amazed if we didn't!

Lulie was twelve and a half when our little sister, Angelina,was still-born. Our mom was very ill afterward, physically and emotionally. I believe other older cousins came to help, but Lulie carried a lot of responsibility on her thin shoulders. (I have clear memories of her braiding my hair in French braids so tight my eyes nearly popped because those braids lasted longer.) Her patience was often thin but looking back, I can understand why—herself to get ready, hair to braid, lunches to pack, homework to keep up with, and housework to do.

When my sister began dating Bud, I saw him as a bit of competition for my big sister's attention. I was seven and she was sixteen. My other sisters and I used to spy on them from upstairs, and once we put a big, blue stuffed monkey in the living room with a bowl of popcorn for them when they came home from a date. (We had named the monkey Treat-a-Popcorn for some unknown reason!)

If Lulie and Bud weren't getting along or if she was having a disagreement with Daddy, we could count on wild, tumultuous piano playing and door slamming as she vented her emotions. Bud and Lulie married in 1960 and took the vacant bedroom my brother, Ron, had left when he married in 1959. Later, they moved to a house on the Bender farm. I missed her terribly and one of my favorite things to do was to visit them.

Lulie made the best spaghetti and meatballs, chocolate chip cookies, and banana cake, and we loved to watch The Three Stooges and I Love Lucy on their television since we didn't have a television at our house.

In 1961, Lulie gave birth to Steve, the first of  three boys. They all became the apple of my eye. I loved going to stay with them for a week to help my sister who soon had her hands full with  three boys in a little over three years. They were adventurous, to say the least, and the fact that they all lived to adulthood was truly miraculous.

I graduated from high school in 1969 and moved to Indiana. That same year, Lulie published a book, *The Outside World*, that in many ways was autobiographical. She had been writing and publishing in Mennonite Sunday School papers for some time, but this was her first book. She and Bud had left the farm and moved to Morgantown, West Virginia, the year before.

Little did we know the heartbreak that was to come the following year as Bud and Lulie's marriage broke up a month or so before Donn and I were to be married. They were both to be in our wedding. The memories of the days and years that followed contained some of those dark stone memories that could still bring me to tears almost fifty years later.

And yet because of the parallel paths their lives followed in the last months that they lived, it's impossible not to believe that in some way, Lulie and Bud were still connected. As we reconnected with their precious boys and some of their families over the past week, reminiscing, laughing, crying, praying and singing, a lot of the sting has been removed from those dark stone memories for me, and I hope for others who were there. For those who couldn't be there, I pray that healing will come as we walk through the days ahead, holding our memories in the light and asking for healing from the One who has already made Bud and Lulie completely whole.

Photos: 1) Lucy Bender, photo taken for her book; 2) l to r Lucy, Mom holding me, Ruthie, Judy; 3) the "girlies" Judy, Ruthie, Daisy; 4) l to r Steve, Nick and Larry, 5) Mike; 6) 1st row l. to r. Mike Bender, Janice Bender (Steve's wife), Ruth, 2nd row Jeff Bender, (Mike's son), Steve Bender, Daisy & Donn, 3rd row: Nick Bender, Harold Yoder (Ruth's husband), Larry & Natalie Beiler

IMTERRUPTIONS?
August 29

Donn and I have an empty nest and live rather orderly lives most of the time. But for the past month or two, things have changed.

At the end of July, our youngest granddaughter's other grandpa (Grandpa Fred) was hospitalized. Since his wife, Grandma Jan, is one-year-old Sarah's regular sitter, we were needed to help care for her while her parents worked. Then Grandpa Fred became very ill and eventually passed away. It was a difficult time for our daughter-in-law and her mom. During those days, Sarah stayed with us around the clock, and her older brother, Connor, was here for a couple of days. Life was not so orderly.

A little over a week later, we received word that my oldest sister, Lucy, was unresponsive in a hospital in Tennessee. We packed and left the next day, Thursday, to make the trip to Chattanooga to be with her and her sons—something we hadn't anticipated when the week began. Once again our schedule was eliminated without a backward glance. Lucy passed away the following Tuesday as we were on our way home.

We unpacked, did laundry, and tried to catch our breath. Even though I knew my life had not been nearly as adversely affected by the happenings of the past month as had the lives of others, I longed for my routine to be restored. When a close friend asked if I was okay, I said, "I just need life to get back to normal."

Later that day, we learned that Sarah's Grandma Jan had broken her hand while her husband was hospitalized but hadn't realized it was broken. She would have surgery on Friday. I remembered what I'd said about needing life to get back to normal and smiled.

I also remembered a devotional I'd read recently. The author had told the Lord she needed to stop having so many interruptions in her life. He responded, "Those interruptions *are* your life." Wow! I needed that reminder. I'm not suggesting we live our every-day lives willy nilly without boundaries or margins, but simply saying when God-ordained interruptions come, we will have more peace and more joy if we recognize them as opportunities rather than seeing them as interruptions.

In retrospect, I wouldn't have missed any of those "interruptions" for anything—time with Sarah, Connor and a friend of his; time with my nephews, some of their families and two of my siblings and their spouses; time to say my goodbyes to my sister—time to be a blessing and to be blessed. *To everything there is a season and a time for every purpose under heaven (Ecclesiastes 3:1).*

Thank you, Father, for the reminder that when interruptions are God-ordained, they *are* my life. Help me to savor and live fully every minute of every interruption you send. Amen.

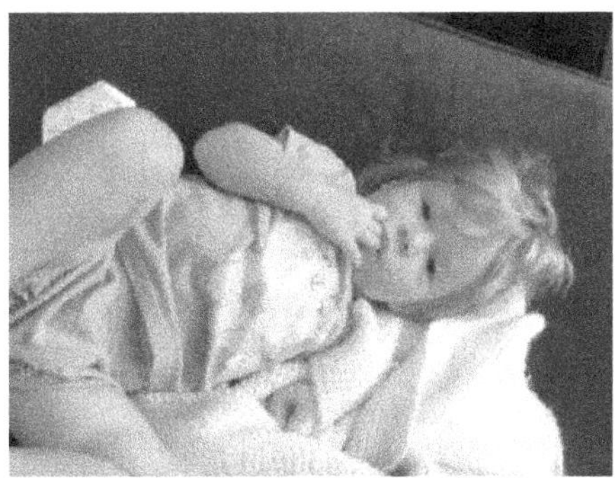

Photo 1) A gift from our daughter, Angelyn 2) Our youngest granddaughter, Sarah

The Outside World
October 4

In the days and weeks that have passed since the death of my sister, Lucy Bender, one of the ways I've honored her is by joining her middle son, Mike, in getting her book into print again. We rejoiced together when he received the first copy this week. Herald Press, a Mennonite publishing company, graciously released us from their copyright so we were free to publish with another company who specializes in this. (The new version is paperback, although eventually it will also be available online as a hardback.)

Lucy's book was originally published in 1969. Technically, the book is fiction. Nevertheless, it is largely autobiographical telling the story of my sister's experiences as a Mennonite teenager attending a high school in "the outside world." (At least one incident mentioned in the book was borrowed from one of our sisters.) Lucy calls herself "Ruth Ann," actually the name of our sister Ruth (Anne with an e), and each of her little sisters are also given different names. I am Donna, the youngest of the "girlies."

My sister was a writer from as far back as I can remember, filling copious sheets with words written by her favorite green fountain pen, Druscilla. Her stories were published in various Mennonite periodicals, copies of which we enjoyed reading after her death. I don't know how she found time to write with her three adventurous boys who were eight, six, and five when her book was published. I suspect the drive to exercise the writing gene, passed down on both sides of our family, gave her little choice.

I didn't fully appreciate Lucy's gift until I read The Outside World again a year or two ago—perhaps to our grandson, Connor. Now that I've spent many years writing and publishing in magazines, periodicals, and more recently books, I have a new appreciation for how well she wrote. As far as I know, she never took writing courses or had any kind of training after high school, but her writing is excellent.

Perhaps the biggest advantage for me in helping Mike with this project was having a closer connection with him than we've had in years. It was a labor of love for both of us that brought us a great deal of satisfaction. The goal was to have the new books finished and available in time for the memorial service that would be held for Lucy and Mark on Saturday, October 13 and that goal was met.

I Peter 4:10 says, *Each one should use whatever gift he has received to serve others, faithfully administering God's grace in its various forms.* I'm so thankful that my sister used the gifts and abilities God gave her to bring honor and glory to Jesus, and I pray that you, too, would make yourself available to use your gifts and abilities for His glory.

OH DEATH WHERE IS THY VICTORY?
October 17

In June when Donn and I went to Maryland for a book signing, we talked with our hostess about the siblings she'd lost. Her family is large and I think she'd already lost three or four brothers/sisters. I told her we had not yet experienced the loss of a sibling in our family, except Angelina who was still born. That conversation stayed with me as I faced the reality that one day, our family would experience our first loss of this sort. I wondered how it would affect us—how we would respond.

Looking back, I believe God was preparing me for what was to come. Even so, the way it came was unexpected. I didn't expect to receive word that one of my siblings was in the hospital, unresponsive and on life support. I didn't expect that the day I'd known would come eventually would come so soon.

Since Lulie was already unresponsive by the time any of us knew she was in the hospital, there were no meaningful conversations, no exchange of last words. Because of this, I was especially thankful that I had purposefully worked through a process of forgiveness and let go of "aughts" I had against others, including my sister, some years earlier. *(If you have aught (the smallest thing) against any, forgive. Mark 11:25)* Although I grieved for what might have been in my sister's life, I wasn't weighed down by personal regrets.

This month many of us dropped everything and went to Maryland for Lulie and Bud's Celebration of Life service. Those who could come reveled in the gift of time with those we love. Not only the siblings but the entire family has been brought closer together. As I evaluate how our family has been affected by this experience, I see the good God has brought.

While we could dwell on the way my sister's life ended, I choose instead to focus on Romans 8:28: *All things work together for good to those who love God, to those who are called according to His purposes.* Because of the circumstances, eleven of us put our lives on hold and went to Tennessee in August, spending more hours together than had been possible for many, many years. This month many of us also dropped everything and went to Maryland for Lulie and Bud's Celebration of Life service.

Perhaps best of all is the realization that regardless of what theological differences my brothers and sisters may have, all of us love Jesus. I have no doubt that one day, all of us will worship together at His feet—probably in four-part harmony! Because of Jesus, who overcame death and the grave, I Corinthians 15:55 is a reality for us and can also be for you.

O death where is thy victory? O grave where is thy sting?

Father, death is part of life that none of us can avoid unless your Son, Jesus, returns before we die. Help us place our trust in Him, not only for this life but also for the life to come. Help us live in such a way that we will be prepared to die. Amen.

Photos: 1) My siblings and me prior to 1959 when Larry was born. 2) My siblings and me and our parents on their 40th wedding anniversary.

GRIEVING
October 25

Grieving is a very individual thing and no two people grieve exactly alike. No two people have exactly the same relationship with the person who passed away. While the deceased may be a "difficult person" for one grieving friend or family member, someone else may have only pleasant memories. Sometimes after the death of a person we've found difficult, there is almost a sense of relief that the difficult relationship is over. In addition, we may feel guilty because we're relieved.

On the other hand, those who longed for a better relationship with the person who died, especially a parent, may grieve because they must face the fact that a better relationship will never happen. Others find themselves dealing with anger they never allowed themselves to experience—anger for things the person did or left undone. It may take a long process to forgive them even though they're gone from this life.

Over all, it's very hard to predict how we will respond when a friend or family member dies. When my sister, Lucy, died, I didn't expect to grieve a great deal because, although we'd been close during some seasons of our lives, we hadn't been close for many years. Then we attended the Celebration of Life service for her and her former husband, Mark, and watched the video her son, Mike, put together. The picture above, taken on Bud and Lulie's wedding day, was in the video. Lulie is looking up at Bud, her sparkling eyes filled with hopes and dreams. Each time I saw the picture, I was reminded of my sister's expectations on that day.

By Thursday of the following week, I couldn't stop thinking about that picture, about how badly the relationship had ended, and I couldn't overcome the sadness that engulfed me.

That afternoon I pressed speed dial to return a call from a friend who'd left me a message. Instead of reaching my friend, Jane, my nephew's wife, Janice, (one person away from Jane on my speed dial) answered! When I got over my astonishment, I ended up telling her how I was feeling and why. She said, "I believe those two (Bud and Lulie) were brought together for a reason, no matter how it ended. And even if that reason was only to give us the three wonderful boys they produced, that was reason enough."

There was nothing she could have said that would have resonated with me more. Janice knows how much I love my nephews and nothing would have convinced me more that, even though my sister's hopes and dreams may not all have been fulfilled, the marriage was worthwhile. My sadness lifted and the sun seemed to shine brighter. We talked for an hour that brought much healing to my soul.

This doesn't mean I won't have other sad days as our family walks through the loss of our first sibling, but the God of all Comfort, who can use even a malfunctioning speed dial to bring us comfort, will see me through. And maybe on another day, He'll use me to comfort you.

Thank you, Father, for the amazing ways you minister to us when our grief is more than we can bear. Thank you for sending the Comforter, the Holy Spirit, who can bring beauty from ashes, the oil of joy instead of mourning. Amen.

Photo: Mark and Lucy (Bud and Lulie) on their wedding day at Springs Mennonite Church.

LET LOVE BE YOUR HIGHEST GOAL
October 31

Some years ago, someone was coming to our house whom I loved dearly but whose actions were breaking my heart. What would I say? What would I do? Should I give her the gifts I'd bought for her and her children? Would I be ruled by love or by my emotions?

When the encounter came, I looked at her with loving eyes. "I hate what you're doing. I hate the example you're setting for your children, but I LOVE you." She wept as I hugged her and gave her the gifts we'd purchased. Letting love be my highest goal (I Corinthians 14:1) and speaking the truth in love (Ephesians 4:15) made it possible for me to remain in relationship with this person whose behavior I abhorred.

As our Country, and even people within the body of Christ, become more and more polarized, speaking the truth in love and allowing love to be our highest goal (I Corinthians 14:1) seems to have become a lost art. Never have I been aware of more things on which people disagree. The question becomes, how can we remain in relationship with family and friends under these conditions—even with those who share our faith in Christ?

The following are some tips I've gleaned from devotionals I've read recently as the Holy Spirit prepared my heart to write on this subject.

- Look for the similarities between you and those around you, rather than looking for the ways you disagree. When you find yourself among people with whom you don't agree, make looking for similarities your focus. Romans 14:19 NIV says, *Let us therefore make every effort to do what leads to peace.* Christ loves and gave His life for those who vote differently than you do. He can enable you to love them too.

- Agree to disagree. This week The Daily Bread featured a wonderful devotional by Mart DeHaan on this subject. He says the apostle Paul suggested ways of finding common ground even under the most polarized conditions in social, political, and religious conflict (Romans 14:5-6). "…the way to agree to disagree is to recall that each of us will answer to the Lord not only for our opinions but also for how we treat one another in our differences." Mr. DeHaan cautions us to remember, "…there are some things more important than our own ideas—even more than our interpretations of the Bible. All of us will answer for whether we have loved one another, and even our enemies, as Christ loved us."

- Acknowledge that even though you may not respect someone else's opinion, you can respect their right to have that opinion. Mr. DeHaan says, "I remember my dad used to talk about how good it is not just to agree to disagree but to do so with mutual love and respect." A couple I know decided that, in order to preserve the relationship, they would never talk about a pecific subject again, respecting each other's right to hold different opinions.There is value in that.

- Avoid controversial subjects in social settings. Is it really necessary to bring up hot topics in a family setting where you know people disagree? Why not look for subjects that won't lead to arguments? If someone else brings up a hot topic, try to steer the conversation in another direction or diffuse the situation with humor.

Marty DeHaan asks the question, "Is it really possible to set aside irreconcilable differences when so much seems to be at stake?" I believe it is. When I'm tempted to distance myself from people whose opinions I dislike, I make this affirmation—silently: "I hate the beliefs you're embracing, the political views you espouse, but I LOVE you." I don't have to love a person's beliefs to love the person.

When making love our highest goal, we can avoid subjects we know will cause dissension and pray fervently for people's eyes to be opened if we think they're being deceived. I'm not suggesting we pretend to agree with wrong interpretations of the Bible or continue going to a church that embraces wrong interpretations. But we don't need to bring up controversial subjects in social settings unless the Holy Spirit prompts us, and we can always choose to speak the truth in love.

Father, please enable us to be patient and kind with those who don't agree with us about anything or everything. Amen. (Mart DeHaan)

A TIME TO SPEAK
November 7

In my previous devotional, I talked about letting love be our highest goal in order to maintain relationships with our loved ones and friends in a polarized culture, even within the body of Christ. However, I clarified that I wasn't suggesting we pretend to agree with wrong interpretations of the Bible or continue going to a church that embraces wrong interpretations. I'd like to elaborate a little more on that today.

When we were foster parents, the CYS director told us the law said children in foster care were to be returned to their biological parents *at all costs*. Later, our foster son's counselor said the law actually stated that *all reasonable efforts* were to be made to return children to the homes of their biological parents. Quite a difference.

In the same way, I'm not suggesting we have a "peace at any price" attitude about maintaining relationships with those we love. The apostle Paul says in Galatians 2:11, *When Peter came to Antioch, I had to oppose him to his face, for what he did was very wrong.* If we are going to be faithful to Christ and His Word, we will undoubtedly find ourselves in situations where it's necessary for us to confront someone for what they're doing or saying, regardless of how dear they may to us.

Recently a friend told us someone quoted scripture in a small group setting. Immediately, someone else responded, "Did Jesus say that or did someone else say that?" We are, indeed, on a slippery slope when we begin to discount the teachings of the Bible unless they are the words of Jesus. Although my friend and many others were shocked, not a single person spoke up.

What hinders us from speaking up in this kind of situation? Fear and intimidation are two of the frontrunners. Perhaps the person speaking has more education than we do or is highly respected. We fear being put down or made to look foolish. I was once a visitor in a Sunday School class being taught by the pastor of the church. He made statements I disagreed with on a subject about which I'm passionate. My heart pounded and my mouth became dry. I couldn't keep silent and be faithful to the truth. When the pastor paused, I said quietly, "I disagree," and respectfully gave my reasons.

When I opened my mouth, I didn't know how I would be treated—if I would be ridiculed, shamed, or condemned for my beliefs. The risk is always there, and we need to be willing to take the consequences if the Holy Spirit is prompting us to take a stand. Erwin Lutzer in his excellent book, "The Church in Babylon" says, *I've heard it said that most college students are not talked out of their faith, they are mocked out of it. Shamed into silence.*

We're living in a day when it's becoming less and less acceptable to disagree with the status quo. In the past, Americans have valued freedom of speech, and the dictum, *I disagree with what you say, but I will fight to the death to defend your right to say it* often ruled. But with the coming of political correctness, that dictum no longer applies.

Here is the irony. The censurers, who are all too ready to deny freedom to those who disagree with them, are perceived by our culture as 'tolerant,' whereas those who express differing views are 'intolerant.' In others words, the philosophy of the left is 'preach tolerance, but practice intolerance against anyone who has the courage to express an opposing point of view.' (The Church in Babylon)

If we're unwilling to risk shame and condemnation for speaking the truth, how will we stand if real persecution comes? May the words of the Lord to Joshua give us courage to take a stand for truth and righteousness at the appropriate time and place.:

Be strong and courageous! Do not be afraid or discouraged. For the Lord your God is with you wherever you go (Joshua 1:9).

WHAT IS A CHEERFUL GIVER?
November 23

Anyone who knew my Grandpa Beiler, fondly called *Grampy,* knew he was a character. It was common knowledge that he was stubborn, headstrong, and never wrong, but I loved him dearly. Once when the hospital had shaved his beard after an accident, he told me I sat on his lap and said, "I love you, Grampy, but you look so ugly without your beard!"

Grampy was a carpenter and had a sawmill and a carpenter shop on his property which he continued to use in spite of failing vision. Every now and then my mother reported in a family letter, "Grampy cut off part of another finger last week." No one was surprised, and we all just shook our heads. I'm not sure how many whole fingers he had left when he died!

But a little over a year ago, I learned something about my irrepressible Grandpa that I'd never known. There was a family-owned grocery store in our town where he loved to go and have lively conversations with the owners. Eloise, one of the daughters of the owners, told me, "Your Grandpa Beiler always planted two gardens every year—one for himself and one to give away. He told us the one he planted to give away always did better than the one he planted for himself."

I love that picture of Grampy's generosity. Rather than only giving away things that he didn't need, he actually planted a garden *specifically* to give away. How easy it would have been for him to decide instead, that which ever garden did better was *his,* and the one that didn't do as well was to give away.

Although Donn's grandfather was also a carpenter, he was about as different from mine as two people could be. But they had at least this one thing in common. When Grandpa Townsend was hospitalized with a

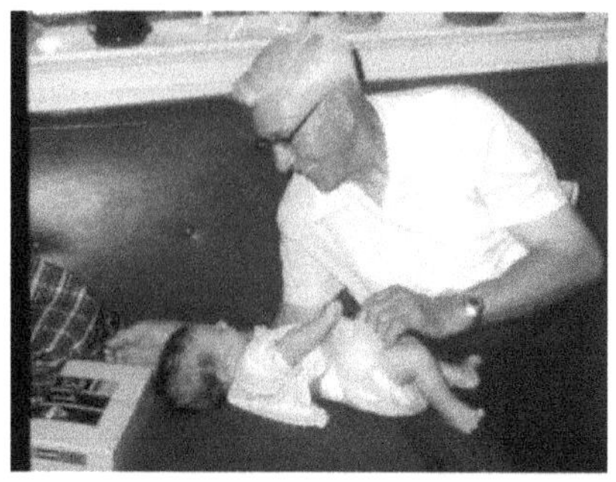

life-threatening heart attack, he asked his daughter to make sure someone took his "tenth money" (already set aside) to put in the offering at church. What an example to his children and grandchildren of obedience and generosity with his finances.

Scripture tells us, "Each man should give what he has decided in his heart to give, not reluctantly or under compulsion, for *God loves a cheerful giver*" (II Corinthians 9:7). I believe both our grandfathers were cheerful givers and examples of the verse that follows, a favorite of mine, *And God is able to make all grace abound to you, so that in all things at all times, having all that you need, you will abound in every good work* (II Corinthians 9:8).

Thank you, Father, for the cheerful givers who have been examples to us of how you want us to live. Amen.

Picture 1) Grampy with his great granddaughter, Diane, and his grandson, Larry. 2) Grandpa Townsend with his great grandson, Robbie.

WHAT THE HEART LOVES
November 29

I've told you before about my struggle to understand how Christians, and people in general, can misinterpret the clear teachings of Scripture pertaining to homosexuality, particularly Romans 1:18-32. Every time I read those words, I shake my head, completely puzzled. However, recently I read a statement that has helped me understand the process that leads to the misinterpretation:

"What the heart loves, the will chooses and the mind justifies.*"

One of the first rules of interpretation of the Bible is this: "Look first for the clear teaching of Scripture, not a hidden meaning. Always try to understand what the author had in mind when you interpret a portion of the Bible. Don't twist verses to support a meaning that is not clearly taught. Unless the author indicates that there is another meaning to what he says, let the passage speak for itself." (Interpret Scripture Accurately website)

Unless the reader is ignoring these rules, looking for a hidden meaning or twisting verses to support a meaning that is not clearly taught, it's impossible to misinterpret Romans 1. Melanchthon's quote helps me understand the process by which the mind can *justify* an interpretation other than the one clearly given. "What the heart loves, the will chooses, and the mind justifies."

It all begins with the heart and what the heart loves. That's why we're told in Proverbs 4:23, *Above all else, guard your heart, for everything you do flows from it*. We must always guard our hearts from loving anything or anyone more than we love the truth. Matthew 6:21 says, *For where your treasure is, there your heart will be also* (Matthew 6:21). The battle has always been and will always be about what your heart loves most, where your treasure is.

There are many things our hearts can love, many things which can become our treasure, which will lead us down the slippery slope to deception. One interesting Scripture in John 12 says many of the people

(*Attributed to Phillip Melanchthon, a colleague of Martin Luther)

of Jesus' day, even the leaders, believed in Jesus but wouldn't confess it because they were afraid of being put out of the synagogue. John says, *They* loved *praise from men more than praise from God*. In our day of political correctness, many who love the praise of men more than the praise of God, embrace unscriptural beliefs because of their fear of retribution and disfavor.

So what about your heart? Are there beliefs and behaviors your will is choosing and your mind is justifying by twisting the clear teaching of God's Word? If so, ask the Lord to reveal what you love and treasure *more* than you love the truth.

Search me, O God, and know my heart: try me and know my thoughts:
And see if there be any wicked way in me (Psalms 139:23-24).

"Truth is so obscure in these times, and falsehood so established, that, unless we love the Truth, we cannot know it." (Blaise Pascal)

WHEN GOD SAYS NO
December 12

In my book, Homespun Faith,, I talked about how God provided my specific desires for a home in Sandy Lake years ago. When we left Sandy Lake to serve as missionaries in Japan, our plan was to live in Sandy Lake when we returned even though we had sold our home there. As our missionary work was coming to an end in 2011, I searched the Internet for weeks for a house in Sandy Lake--a house that would meet our needs in this season of life at a price we could afford. I found nothing.

To my dismay, the home I found that met every criteria I'd asked for was in Greenville, a place I'd always disliked. What was God thinking? The only point in Greenville's favor was that three of our grandchildren lived there.

Seven years later as I sat at a red light on the five-minute trip to Walmart thinking of all the reasons Greenville had been the perfect location for us, I said, "Thank you, God, for not giving us what we wanted."

If God had provided a home in Sandy Lake, we couldn't have done child care before and after school for our grandson, Connor, who lived in Greenville. We wouldn't have been five minutes away from all the home sporting events our sports-minded grandchildren participated in. We wouldn't have been in the same town as Keystone Adolescent Center for whom we did foster care and respite, American Scholar for whom we gave a home to an international student, and Fresh Grounds where I join the Tuesday morning prayer meeting each week to pray for Downtown Ministries.

In the OMS Outreach magazine, Mark Dinnage, OMS Taiwan Field Director, says, *...Michelle and I have often commented how grateful we are that God didn't do what we expected or asked for. What we perceived as God saying no was actually Him saying yes to something even better.*

The same could be said of our experience. God said no to our request for a home in Sandy Lake because He had a better plan for this season. We still love Sandy Lake and still miss our friends there, but we've also come to love Greenville and our new friends here. Even though the years of adjustment were hard, we understand now why God chose to "prepare a place for us" here, and we're so thankful He didn't give us what we asked for!

Heavenly Father, help us trust you
when your answer is no and we don't understand the reason why.
Remind us that you say, *I know the plans I have for us, plans not for evil but for good to give you hope and a future* (Jeremiah 29:11). Amen.

CHRISTMAS MEMORIES
(Purses & Handbags in the Heavenlies)
December 19

My earliest Christmas memories are of going to Grampy Beiler's house on Christmas day to exchange gifts and eat smoked ham that Grampy had smoked in his own smoke house. We lived just down the road from Grampy so it wasn't a long journey.

Interestingly, I don't remember any of the gifts I received, but I will never forget the first year Mama and Daddy gave me money to buy gifts for others. It wasn't much money because we weren't rich, but I stretched every penny so I could buy gifts for my parents, Grampy and the aunties.

I wasn't at all bothered by the fact that I had no money of my own for buying gifts. Since I was dependent on my parents for everything, I didn't think it strange that Mama and Daddy were paying for their own gifts.

It occurred to me today that, in a sense, nothing has changed. All the money Donn and I use to buy gifts is money given to us by our heavenly Father. He's our Provider and even our gifts to Him are given out of what He has given us. Even as an adult, I'm okay with that!

One of my favorite Scriptures is II Corinthians 9:8 NIV. *And God is able to bless you abundantly so that in all things at all times, having all you need, you will abound in every good work.* God blesses us not so we can hoard those blessings, but so that we can bless others. At times, He asks us to sell or give away things that are precious to us to help those in need.

When God was calling us to part with many of our treasures in

2008 prior to returning to Japan, I stumbled over Luke 12:33-34 again and again. I wept and made up my mind that I wanted *...purses and handbags that do not grow old, an unfailing and inexhaustible treasure in the heavens where no thief comes near and no moth destroys.* I wanted to be sure my treasure was in heaven because *...where your treasure is, there your heart will be also* (Amplified Classic). I wanted to remember that everything we have came from God and belongs to Him. Nothing we have here is worth hanging on to and losing our treasure in heaven.

I've lived many years since that first Christmas when my parents gave me money to buy gifts, but I pray I will never forget I have nothing except what has been given to me by my heavenly Father.

Father, help us hold with open hands
all you have given us and never forget that our real treasure is in purses and handbags in heaven. Amen.

REPEAT LESSON FOR SLOW LEARNERS
(For This We Have Jesus)
December 27

In Homespun Faith Volume I, I shared that three Christmas seasons in a row, we or dear friends lost loved ones at Christmas time. Some years later when I asked God why He had allowed these things to happen at Christmas—a time that should be filled with happiness and joy, He told me, "For this, you have Jesus." In other words, it was for times like this that Jesus came.

Recently when we were nearing the beginning of the Advent season, one by one people in leadership at our church became either temporarily or permanently unavailable to plan and orchestrate the special services for this season. In addition, several leaders developed serious, life-threatening illnesses. I, at least, begin to feel like our church family was in a boxing rink receiving one blow after another.

One of our elders said, "Jesus Christ is the cornerstone of the church, and for that reason, we can go on." I'd heard years ago that sometimes the Lord removes the "props" we've been leaning on so we will lean on Him. I'm happy to say that our Church survived that difficult Advent season without most of our props. Many people stepped out of their comfort zones and leaned on Jesus to fulfill roles they hadn't expected to fill. We discovered in a real way that "For this, we have Jesus."

Even though I thought I'd learned that lesson years ago, I discovered when I was tested that I hadn't *really* learned it. Or perhaps I'd learned the lesson in the family arena but not in the church. Thankfully, in God's kingdom, we don't ever really fail a course. In His mercy and grace, He keeps giving us the same test over and over until we pass!

Heavenly Father, plant your truth deep in our hearts so that even when trials come at Christmas or other inconvenient times, we will remember that for this, we have Jesus. Amen.

2019

BEYOND THE WARDROBE
January 10

After Donn and I returned from our first year in Japan, we were asked by Men for Missions, the layman's branch of OMS, to lead a prayer initiative for the nation of Japan. We readily agreed because it would give us the opportunity to pursue our burden and passion to confront the powers of darkness in the nation of Japan, through the power of Jesus Christ, to see the spiritual captives set free.

We knew this kind of prayer isn't widely practiced or understood in the Body of Christ. At one of our MFM meetings for leaders of prayer initiatives, someone expressed frustration that too often the only prayer requests at church prayer meetings were ones that had to do with physical problems. While health problems can certainly be very serious, it seems that prayers that have to do with battling the powers of darkness are seldom encouraged.

A couple years ago, we visited a church in the United States where the Sunday school teacher said he didn't believe we needed to worry about demonic activity in this country. Could it be that's why most of our prayer requests in the church are for health concerns? Are we convinced demonic activity only occurs in the dark corners of Africa? Or do we prefer to believe the battle that rages in the supernatural realm doesn't exist at all? Or that as Christians, we are exempt from these battles?

Some years ago, Ken Dunkerly, CMA missionary to Poland, preached a wonderful message at the Grove City Alliance Church titled, "Beyond the Wardrobe." He compared the supernatural spirit realm to the world of Narnia that lay "beyond the wardrobe." A realm that exists but is invisible to most people.

Rev. Dunkerly said many people simply are not aware, or do not want to recognize, that this supernatural realm exists. But it is *very real*. We agree. About 40 years ago, our eyes were opened to this realm. It was a rude awakening and took us well out of our comfort zone.

We recognized that our battle was against *principalities and powers, and the rulers of the darkness of this world, and against spiritual wickedness in high places.* We saw the need to *Put on the full armor of God* so that we could *take our stand against the devil's schemes* (Ephesians 6:11-12). We discovered *The weapons of our warfare are not carnal but mighty through the power of God to the pulling down of strongholds* (II Corinthians 10:4).

As we wrestled with the new understanding and what it required of us, Donn said one day, "Can't we just live like ordinary people?" We have discovered the answer to that question is no. If we have chosen to be sold-out followers of Jesus Christ, we cannot live like ordinary people.

The realm "beyond the wardrobe" is real. If we choose to ignore it and try to live like ordinary people, we will not only be ineffective soldiers of Jesus Christ, we may end up being casualties. Whether or not we recognize that Ephesians 6:12 is true, all the forces of hell will be aligned against us. We will be soundly defeated or live lives of mediocrity.

Reverend Dunkerly asked us several searching questions repeatedly throughout his message that I'd like to ask you in Part II of this devotional to help you evaluate where you stand in the spiritual battle that's raging.

Father, open our eyes as you opened the eyes of the servant of Elisha to see a clear picture of the battle we face. Enable us to see the enemy clearly, as well as your supernatural intervention. Amen.

BEYOND THE WARDROBE
Part II
January 16

In Beyond the Wardrobe Part I, I told you about Pastor Ken Dunkerly's message, "Beyond the Wardrobe," which compares the supernatural spirit realm to the world of Narnia that lay "beyond the wardrobe." It's a world that is largely invisible, but very real. I also said that unless we recognize and learn how to fight the spiritual battles, we will not only be ineffective followers of Jesus Christ, we may also become casualties.

These are the searching questions Pastor Ken asked us repeatedly during the course of his message:

1) Has your scriptural knowledge been translated into spiritual authority? Many Christians have a wealth of scriptural knowledge but it has never been translated into spiritual authority and has little value in defeating the powers of darkness. How are you using the scriptural knowledge that you have?

2) Have you been changed from a spectator into a participant in the battle that is raging? Or have you chosen instead to attempt to "live like ordinary people"?

If you find yourself lacking in either of these areas, you may ask, *What does it take for our scriptural knowledge to be turned into spiritual authority and for us to be changed from spectators into participants*? I believe step one is to completely surrender our lives to Christ, to *make of our bodies a living sacrifice* (Romans 12:1), being willing to do or go or be whatever and wherever we are led by the Holy Spirit.

It also means turning away from sin, allowing the Lord to do a cleansing work in our life, not harboring any known sin. While refusing to acknowledge the world "beyond the wardrobe" can bring defeat, trying to become a participant in the spiritual battle while still walking in the ways of the world is also very dangerous.

So step one is becoming a sold-out follower of Jesus Christ. This doesn't mean, however, that only "perfect Christians" may step forward to become participants. If that were true, none of us could participate! Paul says in II Corinthians 4:7 NIV, *We have this treasure in jars of clay to show that this all-surpassing power is from God and not from us.* In Zechariah 4:7 NIV, the angel told Zerubbabel, *Not by might nor by power, but by my Spirit, says the Lord Almighty.* Praise the Lord! Each of us is a work in progress, and if God calls us to step up to become a front line participant, He will also prepare us and enable us by His power and His grace.

So where do you stand in the battle that's raging? Has your scriptural knowledge been translated into spiritual authority? Have you been changed from a spectator into a participant? If not, in Part III I want to give you some practical tools to help you make the change.

Heavenly Father, forgive us for being so consumed
with earthly things that we haven't prepared ourselves to fight the
spiritual battles we encounter. Open our eyes to see
the reality of the supernatural battle "beyond the wardrobe,"
and courage to defeat the enemy by your grace. Amen.

GET IN THE GAME
(Beyond the Wardrobe Part III)
January 23

I want to give you some practical tools today to turn your scriptural knowledge into spiritual power so that your can become a participant in the battle that is raging "Beyond the Wardrobe."

Soon after Pastor Dick LaFountain came to the Grove City Alliance Church, he put out copies of *Touch the World through Prayer* by Wesley Duewel. Above it, he put a sign that said, "Free to Intercessors." It has since become a favorite of mine and of my daughter, Angelyn's. I highly recommend it.

Wesley Duewel is a former president of One Mission Society with whom we later served in Japan. For this reason, I was unprepared for the storm that erupted when I suggested presenting teaching from this book to pastors in Japan.

Once again, I recognized that "we wrestle not against flesh and blood, but against principalities, and powers, and spiritual wickedness in high places, and the rulers of the darkness of this world." Satan does not want Christians' scriptural knowledge to be turned into spiritual power, and he certainly doesn't want them to become participants rather than spectators in the battle.

Others have been changed from spectators into participants in the spiritual battle by watching The War Room, an excellent movie that focuses on recognizing and fighting spiritual battles. "Clara" (Karen Abercrombie) reminds me a great deal of my feisty mentor, Frannie, who taught me a great deal about spiritual warfare in my early days. I highly recommend this movie. There's also a book and study guide to go with it.

One word of warning, don't try to fight the battle alone. God didn't call us to be lone rangers. Make sure you're under the umbrella of a godly church or organization if you plan to become a participant in the battle. In 2005, we knew God was calling us to lead a prayer ministry for

Japan but understood our need to be under the umbrella of a godly organization. The next day when we received Men for Mission's call asking if we'd lead their prayer initiative for Japan, it was confirmation of what God had already shown us. This was the protection we'd been looking for.

I'd like to end with a question from Reverend Ken Dunkerley's message, *Beyond the Wardrobe*: "When you come face to face with Satan's activity in your life or in the life of someone else, when demonic forces interfere with your life or the life of someone close to you, are you a fan who stands by to see what's going to happen or are you a passionate player, one who's been prepared to take authority over Satan and all his activity? Are you a spectator, or are you a participant? Are you 'in the game' or are you 'on the bench?'"

If you are "on the bench," I pray these devotionals inspired by Reverend Dunkerley's message will inspire you to ask the Lord what needs to happen in your life so that you can "get in the game." He wants to do all that's needed to prepare you to join the battle.

Heavenly Father, place a longing in our hearts to stop being spectators and be prepared to get in the game! Amen.

Prevailing prayer is prayer that pushes right through all difficulties and obstacles…until spiritual victory is won. (Wesley Duewel)

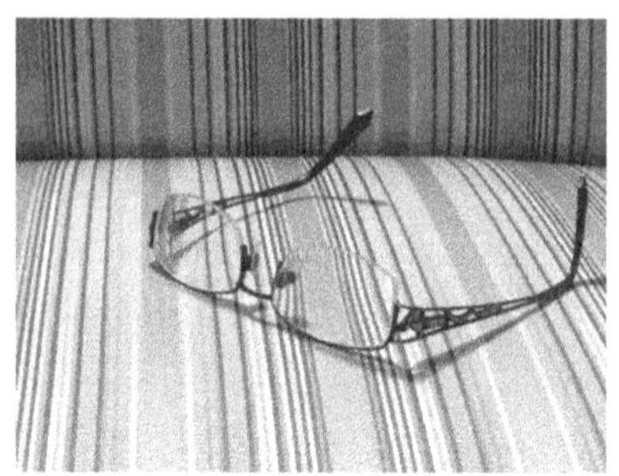

MAKE HIM SMARTER THAN HE IS
February 6

During the Christmas season a couple years ago, I became dizzy and sick every time I bent over to pick up wrapping paper or anything else. The dizziness didn't pass but kept getting worse. Since I had just purchased new glasses, I began to suspect they were the problem. When my eye doctor compared the type of bifocals and type of lenses of the new glasses with my old ones, except for the stronger prescription, they were the exactly same.

At first, he was sure I had an inner ear problem unrelated to my new glasses. After I finally convinced him I could bend over just fine without getting dizzy wearing my old glasses but not when wearing the new ones, he sat and stared at the two pair of glasses. I prayed silently, "Lord, please make him smarter than he is." Not that my eye doctor isn't smart, but I knew he was stumped!

Finally he said, "The slant of the frames of the new glasses is a little bit different than then the old frames." When I asked if he could fix that, he replied that he could. He left the room and returned a few minutes later. We agreed I would wear my old glasses for a few days until my ongoing dizziness had passed, then try the new ones. That's what I did and I had no problems after that.

My doctor said in 35 years of being an eye doctor, he'd never encountered this problem, but God had the solution.

Early this week, Donn and I were wrestling with the challenges of publishing Sarah's Legacy Shared, the second book in my Sarah's Legacy series. I made good notes a year ago when we published book one, but still we ran into new challenges. Tuesday evening when Ingram Spark finally accepted all our files in the first round of validation, I realized that again and again throughout the entire process, God had made us "smarter than we are." He had given us ideas of how to fix each problem when we were stumped or had shown us where to find the answers.

In June of 2017, I went to a series of classes on how to do the work of self-publishing. However, I believe the presenter, who had her own publishing company, had a different agenda—to convince us we couldn't do it ourselves. In the natural, she was probably right—at least in my case. But she had forgotten to figure God into the equation.

Catherine Marshall says when her husband (a pastor) died, the men of the church came to talk to her. They had facts and figures showing why she wouldn't have the finances she and her son needed to live. However, Catherine said, even though supposedly figures don't lie, the men had forgotten to factor God into the equation! How often do we make the same mistake when looking at impossible situations?

In this country self-reliance and independence were highly praised while we were growing up, but God is teaching us that He wants us to rely on Him. The past few days when Donn was stumped while working on photo shop issues that are far outside my skill set, I cried out to God again and again. "Father, you know I have no idea. Please show him what to do. Please help him." In other words, make him smarter than he is. My frustration turned to faith as God answered again and again.

Do you have an impossible situation in your life? I challenge you to ask our heavenly Father to make you, or someone who can help you, smarter than you/they are!

Father, forgive us for so often forgetting to figure you into the equation when looking at impossible situations. Only you have the ability to make us smarter than we are! Amen.

LIVING OUR EPITAPH
February 22

Years ago our Sunday School teacher told us he and his wife had ordered their headstone from a local merchant who had completed the etching on it except the dates of their deaths. The dealer asked if he could keep it for awhile to display it. Gene agreed, assuming that the store owner wanted to display it in his shop. A few weeks later, Gene was more than a little surprised to see their tombstone on the back of a pickup truck parked by the curb in Sandy Lake!

Can you imagine suddenly stumbling upon a headstone with your name on it in the center of town? How would you feel? What epitaph do you think you would find if it had been chosen by your loved ones? Would you be happy with the inscription or would it prompt you to reassess your life?

I don't remember whether Gene and his wife had chosen an epitaph for their tombstone—only that he was startled to find the headstone displayed in the center of town.

Charles Stanley says he likes to walk through cemeteries and read the epitaphs. He says it's interesting to read the words that have been chosen to sum up a person's life and a helpful way to reassess one's own life.

We're each going to leave a testimony of some kind when we die. Have you ever wondered what your loved ones will remember about you? What words do you want inscribed on your gravestone? (Charles Stanley)

I think this is a subject worth considering. We will all leave a testimony when we die, whether good or bad. Our friends and loved ones will have memories that will either be a blessing or a curse. All of us have done things we regret but as long as we have breath, we have the opportunity to create new memories or ask forgiveness for the pain we've caused.

We can't control what loved ones would inscribe on our tombstone, but we can ponder what words we would choose if the choice were ours. *For me to live is Christ, to die is gain (Philippians*

1:21) is the verse that came to mind as I considered what words I might choose for my tombstone. Knowing that my faith will have become sight by the time the date of my death is inscribed on my tombstone is an awesome thought.

Years after my father's death, I listened to a cassette tape of a message he'd preached in the small Mennonite Church he pastored. After the singing of the last verse of Amazing Grace, he said, *"When we've been there ten thousand years, bright shining as the sun, we've no less days to sing God's praise than when we've first begun.* Can you imagine what that will be like?" I rejoiced because I knew that he now knows what it's like to sing God's praises in that wonderful place. One day I will join him, and I will know in reality that *To live is Christ, and to die is gain.*

Father, forgive us when we've failed to live
up to the sort of epitaph we would want inscribed on our tombstone.
Help us live in such a way that we wouldn't be ashamed to see it
displayed in the center of town. Amen.

CHECKING THE POWER SWITCH
March 20

Last week I thought my Kindle wasn't working. I had plugged it into a charger the night before that we keep continually plugged into a power strip. The next morning, it had not charged. What could be wrong?

After fiddling for a few minutes, I noticed that no orange light glowed from the outlet switch to indicate the outlet I used was turned on. There was nothing wrong with my Kindle. The problem was that, inadvertently, the power to the outlet had been turned off. As soon as I flipped the switch, the icon appeared to tell me the Kindle was charging.

As I stared at my Kindle, I wondered how often in life we think there's something wrong with our marriage, our job, our life in general when the real problem is that inadvertently, we have turned off the power.

It can happen so subtly—we allow ourselves to be offended by something our spouse says or does. A few days later, something else happens that rubs us the wrong way and before long, everything they say and do irritates us. We find ourselves snapping at them, our children, our co-workers, wondering all the while what's wrong with *them.*

Or perhaps a temptation from our past rears its ugly head and we yield to it until it again becomes a besetting sin. Once again, we wonder why nothing in our lives is going right. Psalm 66:18 says, *If I regard sin in my heart, the Lord will not hear me.* Looking at our sin, recognizing that it's there, and doing nothing about it is one way of turning off the power.

However, I John 1:9 NIV tells us, *If we confess our sins, He is faithful and just to forgive us our sins and cleanse us from all unrighteousness.* We're also told, *Confess your faults one to another and pray for one another that you may be healed"* (James 5:16 NIV*).* Some tenacious sins may not lose their grip until we've confessed them to another person. God knows we need the prayers of our Christian brothers and sisters to get free.

Sometimes life is simply hard for no reason, but it's never inappropriate to check the power switch.

Thank you, Father, that even when we're the ones responsible for turning off the power, you are longing to forgive us and restore it once again. Amen.

PUTTING OFF AND PUTTING ON
April 4

But now you also put off all these: anger, wrath, malice, blasphemy, filthy communication out of your mouth (Colossians 3:8 KJV).

As we near the Easter season, we're reminded that Jesus died to take the punishment for our sins to remove the barrier between us and God. What a wonderful gift He gave us! However, we are also told in Colossians 3:8, *Put off anger, wrath, malice, blasphemy, and filthy communication out of your mouth.* So even though we've been forgiven and restored to right relationship with God, apparently we have a part to play in "putting off" our sins. How exactly do we do that?

Years ago when I was wrestling with being consistently obedient in one area of my life, our pastor introduced me to the concept of "spiritual affirmations." He suggested I come up with an affirmation that reflected my choice to obey God in this area and repeat it each day. Why do we need to do it each day? Because the first time we send that message to our sub-conscious, a little guy down there will respond, *"No Way!"* We have to keep sending the message until that little guy believes we are serious about obedience.

I've used many spiritual affirmations over the years, including the strategy of "Putting Off." As I washed the dishes or drove to an appointment, I would begin the ABC's of this affirmation: "I put off anger, bitterness, criticizing, envy, fear, guilt, hatred, irritability, jealousy…" or whatever the Holy Spirit brought to mind for each letter of the alphabet. It was an effective way to send the message to my inner being that I was choosing to get rid of each sinful character trait.

In the accompanying "Putting On" strategy, I used the qualities we're told to *put on* in verse twelve of Colossians three as though I were putting on articles of clothing: "I put on compassion, gentleness, humility, kindness, patience and over all those, love." (Alphabetical order was easier to remember.) Once again I sent the message to myself that emulating these qualities was my choice. I was cooperating in a Holy Spirit make over!

Change is never easy, but if we are serious about putting off the old and putting on the new, I believe the Holy Spirit will give us creative ways to participate in the process. It always begins with a choice.

Thank you, Father, that as we choose to cooperate with the Holy Spirit, you work in us both to will and to do your good pleasure (Philippians 2:13).

I'M JUST INTO GOD
May 1

"You're really into the Bible, aren't you?" Our seven-year-old foster daughter sounded a tad scornful.

When I agreed that I *was* really into the Bible, she responded loftily, "I'm just into God."

My reply was quick and to the point. "If you're into God, you'd *better* be into the Bible. Otherwise, people can tell you anything they choose about God, and you won't know if it's true or not."

I'm so thankful for the godly foundation I was given in the Christian home where I was raised. Although none of us live out the truth perfectly, my parents' deep respect for God's Word had a lasting impact on my life.

However, when we got to Japan, I discovered that many people had no knowledge of the Bible or no reason to be impressed if I told them what I was teaching was in the Bible. One man who came to our English Bible study argued and debated every truth we presented. At last he said, "If only you would agree that the Bible is a myth, then we could have common ground."

Another dear lady who had been listening to Bible teaching in English class for a long time told me, "I believe in Jesus but I don't believe Mary was a virgin." I explained that I believed it because it was in the Bible. I said, "Everyone has to decide whether or not they believe the Bible is true. There are many historical proofs that Jesus existed and that the Bible *is* true, but each person must decide for herself." Soon after, she became a Christian and was baptized.

Sadly, I'm afraid the lives of many Christians show that while they may be "into God," they are definitely *not* into the Bible—at least, not if that means reading and obeying it. Occasionally I hear people say, "I believe every word in this Book." The truth is they would be hard pressed to tell you anything that "Book" says.

Charles Stanley says, "If we aren't grounded in Scripture, we'll unknowingly accept philosophies and teachings that will lead us astray. But when biblical truth has saturated our mind and heart, we'll sense a

186

red flag pop up in our spirit whenever we encounter an erroneous concept."

One of the people God brought into our lives in Japan had been involved in a false religion. After she received Jesus, her past erroneous beliefs would often come out in conversation—her belief in reincarnation, for example. My standard mantra became, "It's not in the Bible." Her surprise was always evident as she processed a new set of beliefs. Thankfully, she responded by getting into God's Word and learning for herself what it said. She was not just into God, she was into the Bible.

How about you? If someone were to evaluate your life to determine whether you are into the Bible or just into God, what would they find?

Father, forgive us when we neglect your Word.
Forgive us when we act as if we can be *into* God without being *into* the Bible." Give us a hunger for the truth so we won't be deceived by false prophets and doctrines when they come. Amen.

IS YOUR BEAUTY ONLY SKIN DEEP?
May 16

I remember the day I realized I was no longer the youngest or the most slender woman at the place where I worked. Soon afterward at a family reunion, I became aware that I no longer had those distinctions there either. The natural process of growing older accounted for the first and the weight gain came from a medicine I needed to function well. As often happens, I didn't realize how much I depended on my youth and my slender figure for my identity until they were gone.

Not everyone, however, is unaware of this connection. I heard an account of a beautiful young lady being asked by an older gentleman, "What gives you such self-confidence?" She replied, "It's because I'm young and beautiful." The man responded, "I'm sorry to hear that." When she asked him why, he answered, "Because one day your youth and your beauty will be gone. Then what will you base your confidence on?" A very good question.

I was saddened recently to see an actress whose beauty had been marred by far too many face lifts. Perhaps actors and actresses place their confidence in their physical appearance even more than most. But regardless of our role in life, it is so important to learn at an early age that we are made in the image of God and our worth and value come from Him. We are not more or less valuable because of our age, weight, appearance, abilities, or position in life.

I've heard it said that we should never compliment our children and grandchildren more on their physical attractiveness or athletic ability than we do on their positive character traits. We don't want to contribute to them basing their identity on physical qualities that will fade rather than on character traits that will last forever. I am more apt to send a note of encouragement to our grandchildren when they've shown great strength of character than when they've won a medal.

In one of my favorite devotional books, Life Promises for Women, Cynthia Heald says in her introduction: *In this book you will find stories of women from varied walks of life who portray qualities of inner beauty and character. My prayer is that the lives of these women and the Scriptures given will challenge and encourage you to claim not only the promises of God but His teachings as well so that you will be clothed with the beauty that comes from within—the 'unfading beauty of a gentle and quiet spirit' (I Peter 3:4).*

If our beauty is only skin deep, aging will be an excruciating process. We will increasingly believe the lies of Satan and our culture that our worth and value is gone rather than believing that our worth and value come from the One in whose image we're formed.

Father, help me realize that I will only walk in true beauty if the beauty of Jesus shines through me. Amen.

Charm is deceptive, and beauty is fleeting; but a woman who fears the lord is to be praised (Proverbs 31:30 NIV).

SITTING ON THE BENCH
May 20

Have you ever had a season in your life when you felt like you were sitting on the bench watching other "players" who had more active roles in the game of life? Did you feel left out and worthless—of little or no value?

Donn and I enjoy watching baseball and over the past few months, the Pittsburgh Pirates have had a plethora of players on the disabled list, including Corey Dickerson. He had been unable to play for so long we'd almost forgotten about him.

Then one evening a rookie who had just hit a home run, ran back to the dugout and hugged Corey and shouted, "I love you, man!" The broadcasters told us that the camera man had to wait for the rookie earlier in the day because he and Corey were having an intense discussion in the locker room.

Later in the evening when they interviewed another young player who is having a phenomenal season after a miserable previous year, he said, "Kudos to Corey Dickerson for getting me back on track." The next day another young player gave credit to Corey for the success he was having.

We were amazed. While Corey was "sitting on the bench," he was not licking his wounds feeling sorry for himself, he was investing in the lives of young players, helping his team even while unable to play. One of the rookies said, "It's impossible to place a value on that kind of player. It's huge."

So what about us? Can we also choose to invest in the lives of others while "sitting on the bench" whether due to ill health or simply due to the season we're in? I believe we can—whether through prayer, words or notes of encouragement, or words of wisdom at a critical time.

Years ago when I was going through a devastating season, an elderly retired pastor, who was mainly "sitting on the bench," spoke words of encouragement to me at church one day. His words gave me courage to get up and try again. I can't put a value on the words he spoke and the impact they had on my life, but it was huge.

So if you are in a season of bench sitting, continue to make yourself available to God. Ask Him to show you how you can make a difference in the lives of those who are playing a more active role. Above all, refuse to give in to self-pity because of what you are unable to do.

Father, help us to recognize that we still have value even while "sitting on the bench," and that you can still use us if we make ourselves available to you. Amen.

To everything there is a season and a time to every purpose under heaven (Ecclesiastes 3:1.).

THE GIFT OF LIFE
June 5

My mother told me years ago that I spent the first afternoon of my life trying to die. She said I was born with the umbilical cord wrapped around my neck three times, and it was a miracle that I lived. I was intrigued by the fact that she didn't say I was fighting to live but that I was trying to die.

Years later I realized this had become a pattern in my life. When things became difficult, my tendency was to give up, sometimes wishing I didn't have to go on living. I battled depression, insecurity, fear and guilt, and at one of my lowest points, I begged God to let me die.

I remember the dark night of the soul when I finally said, "God if you won't let me die, would you teach me how to live?" I can't say that immediately my life became all sunshine and roses, but it was a turning point. Little by little, the Holy Spirit taught me the truths I needed to be set free. He guided me to Christian books, using them to train me in healthier living. He blessed me with Christian counselors who helped me recover. And He revealed and freed me from hidden sins, conforming me more and more to the image of Christ.

Many times I've told struggling clients and friends, "I can honestly say I'm glad I went through the things I did because otherwise, I would have nothing to say to you. I wouldn't know how to help you."

God spared my life again on the day of our children's birth. The next day someone working in my hospital room said, "We almost lost you yesterday." My nurse gave her a dirty look, apparently not wanting me to know, but it was unnecessary because I already knew.

Every mother's day, I give God thanks for the privilege of being a mother, the privilege of helping my husband raise our twins and invest in the lives of many other children through foster care, as well as in the lives of our grandchildren.

As I write this, I am celebrating my 68th birthday. How thankful I am that in God's providence, twice He gave me the gift of life when I could easily have died. I am so aware that each day I live is a gift from

God. During these sixty-eight years, I've not only had the privilege of becoming a daughter of the King, but I've had the privilege of loving Him, serving Him, and allowing His light to shine through me.

When I think of all God has done for me, a song by Chris Tomlin best expresses my feelings:

How can I keep from singing Your praise?
How can I ever say enough
How amazing is Your love?
How can I keep from shouting Your name?
I know I am loved by the King
And it makes my heart want to sing.

If you are going through a dark night of the soul, perhaps you could also ask Jesus to teach you how to live. He knows you better than you know yourself, and He knows exactly what you need to make your life worth living.

Father, how thankful I am for the gift of life, for experiencing your love and your grace. I pray your intervention for those going through deep waters, that they too could experience the gift of a life lived for you.
Amen.

CHOOSING TO TRUST
June 20

About four months ago, I took my five-year-old keyboard to an electronic repair shop for an estimate. I'd been told by Marks Music that it might cost more to fix than it was worth, and this repair shop was the only place who fixed them. The man at the repair shop said they'd call me with the estimate, but they never called. Every time I called them or went in to the shop, I was told, "I'm going to get to that this week," or "I'm trying to find out if the parts are still available," or some similar story.

On my birthday, I complained about the situation to our son, only expecting sympathy. Robb listened and then said, "I'll go pick it up for you."

I'm sure I looked puzzled as I answered, "Okay, but what will I do then?"

"I'll either fix it or we'll find someone who can."

Robb is good at fixing computers, but as far as I knew, he'd never attempted to fix a musical instrument. Although my default setting would have been to question him or object, he seemed so confident that he could do it that I gave him the "stub" that would allow him to pick up my keyboard. I sensed the Holy Spirit prompting me to trust him.

As good as his word, Robb texted me the next day to tell me he'd picked up the keyboard. There was little the man could say since I'd been waiting for almost three months. I was thankful Robb had stepped in so I wouldn't have to deal with that part of the situation. A few days later I showed our son what the problem was since the keyboard worked fine except in the Accompaniment Mode—the mode I always used.

Robb went online and found a manual (a lot of pages were missing from the one I gave him) and contacted Casio to ask questions. They responded with questions which he passed along to me. I had no idea at first what they were talking about but when Robb directed me to the correct pages in the online manual, one phrase jumped out: Full Range Keyboard. The wheels in my brain began to turn. I called Robb. "I think the problem is that I've forgotten a step in setting up the keyboard to play it in the Accompaniment mode I'm used to—Full Range Keyboard. I can't remember quite how to do it, but I think I can figure it out."

Robb responded, "I know exactly how to do it. I saw it in the manual."

He still had the keyboard at his house so a few days later when we went to pick up our granddaughter, Sarah, Robb read me the steps to get the keyboard into Full Range Keyboard Accompaniment mode. When I experimented, everything worked perfectly. Without his help, I probably would have ended up buying a new keyboard because no one else had taken the time to help me figure out what the real problem was.

A few days before my birthday, I'd been thinking about growing older and about the possibility that the time might come when I wouldn't have Donn to depend on. What would I do? The thought of having to do life without my husband created fear.

Although I didn't express this fear to anyone, not even God, the Lord knew my thoughts. I believe He orchestrated this keyboard situation at just the right time to show me that He would provide someone on whom I could depend if I would trust Him. I'm in awe of a Heavenly Father who knows how to calm my fears when I've barely recognized them myself.

So don't be anxious about tomorrow. God will take care of your tomorrow too. Live one day at a time (Matthew 6:34 TLB).

WHICH VOICE WILL YOU CHOOSE?
July 3

Last week I had the privilege of calling some members of my high school graduating class. One of the people I talked with had been married to a cousin of mine until she passed away several years ago. I didn't know my cousin well but knew she'd had a serious illness even before they married.

My classmate told me how people discouraged him from marrying her because of her illness. He reiterated the fears people had of what would happen if he married her, and then told me, "We had forty wonderful years together. We couldn't have biological children but she meant more to me than a dozen children." He is so thankful he chose not to give in to fear.

This reminded me of the day my Uncle Irvin's wife, Tillie, told me people didn't think Uncle Irvin should marry her because she was six years olde.. She said they were afraid she would die and he'd be left to raise their children alone. (I couldn't help laughing since Aunt Tillie was now in her late nineties and my uncle had passed away many years earlier!) Uncle Irvin had also chosen trust over fear and received the blessing of a godly wife who loved him and helped him raise their seven children.

And then there is our children's long-time friend, Dwight, who wrestled with whether or not it was fair to marry when he was on dialysis and needed a kidney transplant. I imagine he and Christy, the woman he loved, also were told all the reasons they shouldn't marry.

After a great deal of prayer and soul searching, they too chose faith over fear. We were present when a police officer arrived at their wedding reception to tell Dwight a kidney, which turned out to be a perfect match, was waiting for him in Pittsburgh. Almost twenty one years later, I am still in tears at God's wonderful affirmation of their choice of faith over fear.

If we choose to follow Jesus, each of us will have many opportunities to make a choice between fear and faith. Many voices will call out to us, trying to distract us from listening to the Voice of Truth, but we, too, can choose which voice we will listen to, which voice we will obey. I love the lyrics written in The Voice of Truth by Mark Hall.

Chorus

But the voice of truth tells me a different story
The voice of truth says, "Do not be afraid!"
The voice of truth says, "This is for My glory"
Out of all the voices calling out to me
I will choose to listen and believe the voice of truth

Father, forgive us for the many times we've chosen fear over faith, for the many times we have not listened and obeyed the Voice of Truth. Fill us with faith and perfect love that drives out fear. Amen.

AUTUMN
July 18

On Friday morning, July 12, 2019, at 11:00 a.m., the First Presbyterian Church was filled to honor the life of a ninety-six-year-old woman who didn't know a soul when she came here thirty years ago.

Autumn Colby, a pharmacist from Pittsburgh, had headed for Erie looking for a place to retire. Downtown Ministries, First Presbyterian Church, and all who knew her will be eternally grateful that someone convinced her that Saint Paul's Senior Living Community in Greenville had everything she wanted.

Everyone chuckled when her pastor told us he had never had more instructions about how to do a service than he'd had with this one! He had four bullet points to guide his meditation:

1. Speak a clear word of the gospel of Jesus Christ.

2. Announce often the amazing grace of God.

3. Lift up Jesus Christ as the only way of salvation

4. Don't take too long!

And one last instruction that made me laugh and cry: *Talk about Autumn over the lunch table; in the sanctuary, talk about Jesus.*

Autumn was in the prayer group that was the foundation of Downtown Ministries twenty five years ago and still there when I joined the group about eighteen years later. How thankful I am that God gave her the gift of long life.

As I got to know her, I never ceased to be amazed at Autumn's refusal to allow her age to keep her from being involved with life. One Tuesday morning when we met for prayer at Fresh Grounds, I noticed she looked a little sleepy and asked her teasingly, "What time did you go to bed last night?"

In a small voice, she responded, "1:00."

"1:00! What were you doing up at 1:00 in the morning?"

"Making tea cakes for the church."

I laughed, shook my head and said, "I'm a good bit younger than you, but *I* don't even stay up until 1:00 a.m. making tea cakes for the church!"

Autumn admitted she also often stayed up half the night reading because once she got started, she couldn't stop. Then she added, "But I can't go into my bedroom during the day." When I asked her why not, she said, "Because my bed calls my name real loud!"

Her sense of humor was one of the things I loved most about Autumn. One day at prayer meeting, Marty Johnson, Director of Downtown Ministries, was talking about the new defibrillator Fresh Grounds had purchased which can prevent sudden death. Autumn looked at him sternly and said, "DO NOT use that thing on me!" Amidst the laughter, we all knew Autumn would live out her life of service to the Lord but did not want to remain on earth one moment longer than necessary.

After I received the news of Autumn's passing, I grieved because I hadn't gotten to say good bye. Then I remembered that every Tuesday when we were both at prayer meeting, I walked to her car with you (yes, she was still driving), tucked her in on her big cushion, kissed her cheek and told her I loved her. I *had* told her good bye in the way that probably meant the most to her.

Unlike the ninety-year-old man who said, "If I had known I would live twenty five years after retirement, I would have spent my time doing something besides perfecting my golf swing," Autumn spent her retirement investing in the Kingdom. Only heaven will show the harvest that resulted from her investment.

Father, thank you for Autumn's life and for the example she set of how to spend one's retirement years. Give us grace to follow her example to live our entire life, including our retirement, investing in your Kingdom. Amen.

EVERY PROMISE IN THE BOOK IS MINE?
August 15

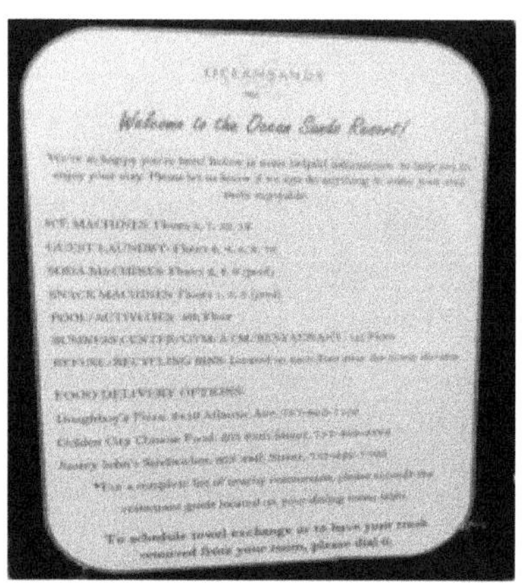

This year we decided to look for an AirBnB at Virginia Beach for our vacation. The condo we rented was small and not luxurious but our bedroom had a balcony that overlooked the ocean. I could hear the waves lapping if I left the sliding glass doors open. It was perfect!

Our condo was located in a resort, but since it was through AirBnB, we weren't sure what conveniences we were entitled to. A large sign on the refrigerator indicated that daily housekeeping would not be done. All week we used the same two sets of towels and wash cloths provided, and all week Donn carried our garbage to the Refuse and Recycle receptacles near the elevator.

On the last day of vacation, I read the "fine print" at the bottom of the *Welcome to the Ocean Sands Resort* sign hanging on our refrigerator. (It was beside the sign with the larger print that said *No Housekeeping*.) The fine print said, *To schedule towel exchange or to have your trash removed from your room, please dial 0.* I groaned. It was too late now, but we could have had clean towels every day instead of using the same two sets all week. We could also have had our trash removed instead of carrying it out ourselves.

In the total scheme of things, no real harm was done because we didn't understand the privileges that were ours. We still bathed and got rid of our garbage! However, it made me wonder how often Christians suffer unnecessarily because they don't understand the privileges that are ours in Christ.

Oh what peace we often forfeit
Oh what needless pain we bear

All because we do not carry
Everything to God in prayer.
(What a Friend We Have in Jesus)

Just as we didn't read the "fine print" on the sign on our refrigerator, many Christians don't take the time to read God's Word regularly and become familiar with the promises there…promises they can never claim because they don't know what they are. The best decision I ever made (around age 25) was to read God's Word every day. I can't imagine how differently my life might have turned out if I'd never made that choice.

One of my favorite memories is of my mother sitting in our living room reading her Bible. Little did she know that later in life, she would suffer from macular degeneration and would no longer be able to read God's promises. But nothing could rob her of the words stored up in her heart from the hours she'd spent reading God's Word.

I pray you won't neglect one of the most valuable treasures God has given us, the treasure of His Word. II Peter 1:4 NIV tells us, *He has given us His very great and precious promises, so that through them you may participate in the divine nature and escape corruption in the world caused by evil desires.* Wow! I don't know about you, but I want to claim every promise that will enable me to participate in the divine nature because my human nature leaves much to be desired. But the choice is ours.

Father, enable us to make choices that will fill us with your Word and all the great and precious promises it contains. Show us how to claim your promises and make them our own. Amen.

WE DO NOT LOSE HEART
August 29

On August 17, 2019, the Northern High School Class of 1969 celebrated our 50th Class Reunion. How can that be? In some ways, it seems like only yesterday we walked the halls at Northern thinking that graduation would *never* come. In other ways, when I think of all that has happened, it seems as if a century has passed.

Some people avoid this sort of milestone because it reminds them of the inevitable—we're getting older. Others become sentimental and come to their fiftieth class reunion for the first time since graduating. No matter how one reacts, there is no turning back the clocks—we are all fifty years older than we were when we graduated.

My sweet husband tells me I still look the same as I did when he married me forty-nine years ago. Many of my classmates at the reunion told me they didn't need to look at my name tag because I still look the same.

In spite of that, when I look in the mirror, I see the changes. I've never felt the need to dye my hair because I inherited my father's genes, but I still have plenty of gray hair. I don't have many wrinkles on my face but plenty on my neck, where one's age will always show. And some days when cold weather comes, my aches and pains make me feel older than my sixty-eight years.

Since aging is inevitable, how do we face the process? How do we face our mortality? II Corinthians 4:16 NIV tells us, *Therefore, we do not lose heart. Though outwardly we are wasting away, yet inwardly we are being renewed day by day.*

When we were young, many of us placed a great deal of emphasis on our appearance. If we've never learned that inner beauty is of much more importance than outer beauty, our mirror will have the power to devastate us as we age. In her meditation on Cultivating Beauty,* Cynthia Heald says, *Just as a woman's lack of inner character can mar her good looks, a beautiful soul can render a plain face lovely.* The same is true for a man.

Uncommon beauty is sown and cultivated in the soul. It is watered by passion and wisdom, it puts down deep roots by practicing integrity, it flourishes by being selfless and gracious to others, it grows strong by staying firmly planted in its circumstances and courageously enduring the clouds and the wind...It is this extraordinary priceless beauty that we want—all the spa treatments in the world cannot keep us young or make us truly beautiful. *

In truth, outwardly we *are* wasting away. We have no choice about that. But we can choose to be inwardly renewed day by day through God's Word and through choosing to *clothe ourselves...with the beauty that comes from within, the unfading beauty of a gentle and quiet spirit, which is so precious to God (I Peter 3:4 NIV).*

It is Marie Stoops' opinion that, *You can take credit for beauty at sixteen. But if you are beautiful at sixty, it will be your soul's own doing.* I'm not sure I agree since even at sixteen, a great deal of credit for beauty belongs to God who created us, but by the age of sixty, how we've lived our lives will likely add or detract from beauty.

If you find that looking in the mirror is causing you to lose heart as you age, make a conscious decision to change your focus. Spend more time and money on reading God's Word and inspirational books that emphasize inner beauty than you do on cosmetics and anti-aging cream. Ask God to show you how to be inwardly renewed day by day.

*From the book *Life Promises for Women*

Heavenly Father, make whatever changes are needed so that the beauty of Jesus can shine through us. Clothe us with the beauty that comes from within, the unfading beauty of a gentle and quiet spirit, which is so precious to you. Amen.

HOW DOES HE WANT YOU TO USE IT?
September 11

Running footsteps followed the lilting, "Hi" that preceded the blonde, brown-eyed sprite of nine who dashed up the side-walk toward us a few evenings ago. Natalie lives two streets over, and we've never met her parents or the rest of her family. But if she catches a glimpse of Donn and me out on our evening walk, she races over for a hug and a chat.

Shivers of joy run through me when I hear her sweet voice. Or the precious voices of Kylee and Liam, the six-year-old twins who live catty-corner across the street, who also come running for hugs if they spot us when we leave the house. They love eating Donn's banana bread—and aren't shy about asking him to make them some—and listening to me read stories.

I can't remember a time when I didn't love children—it began before I was grown up myself. I loved going to my oldest sister's house to help take care of my nephews and, later, babysitting for the children of our friends when we were newly-weds. The daughter of a friend of mine told me after I'd been interacting with her children one day, "I can tell from watching you that you were created to be with kids."

Before Donn and I married, I wanted at least four children (Donn wanted three), but when I almost died when our twins were born, we decided they needed a mother more than they needed a brother or sister. In spite of this fact, God has found ways to bring children into our lives in every season.

Neighborhood children came to our home in the housing development in Penn Hills and would have stayed all day if I hadn't sent them home. I held Bible Clubs and we also taught children's church at the Free Methodist Church we attended there. Later, we had a Christian Nursery School in Sandy Lake and taught CYC at the Wesleyan Church. We also worked with children in various capacities at the Lakeview United Methodist Church and did foster care for the Mercer County CYS and later, Keystone Adolescent Center.

Angi always used to beg for a big sister but I told her it was impossible because she and Robb were our first children. Years later when God brought Jennifer, who is a year older than our kids, into our family, I remembered Angi's desire. How blessed we've been to have her and her family as part of ours.

And then, of course, there's our six awesome grandchildren. We had the privilege of providing before- and after-school childcare for Connor, the next to the youngest one, because God brought us to Greenville. And then there is Sarah, the youngest that came along after I'd been told, "We're done, Mom. You'll have to wait for the greats." What great joy all our grandchildren have brought us. This youngest one, coming when the next youngest was 12 and a half, has been a special blessing because I was really missing this younger age.

I'm so thankful that even though circumstances deprived me of having more than two biological children to love, God had a plan to give me children to love in every season of my life in one way or another. He is never caught off guard if our plans are thwarted by circumstances beyond our control.

One of my favorite lines from The Sound of Music goes something like this: Reverend Mother to Maria, "God has given you a great capacity to love. Now we have to find out how He wants you to use it."

If God has given you a great capacity to love some particular group of people—children, the elderly, prison inmates, teenagers, etc. and it seems the door is closed to using it, keep your eyes fixed on Jesus. If the gift is truly from Him, He will provide opportunities to use that gift even though it may not be in the way you had planned.

Father, your Word tells us *Every good and perfect gift is from above, coming down from the Father of Lights* (James 1:17 NIV). The capacity to love a particular group of people is an awesome gift. Help us to recognize the gift and the opportunities you give us to use it. Amen.

Go Light Your World
October 9

Last summer one of our neighbors set a large ceramic pig out on their property at the corner of Plum Street and First Avenue. Immediately it gained fame as "the Plum Street Pig." It was so much fun and such a great conversation piece that I began to wrack my brain for something we could set on the front corner of our property. As we visited flea markets and department stores, I was constantly on the look out for the perfect lawn ornament.

Eventually, my search evolved into looking for something that would be, in some way, symbolic. One day a light bulb came on in my brain… of course, a lighthouse It would be the perfect symbol of what we wanted to be in our neighborhood—a light to help draw our neighbors to Jesus.

Simultaneously, as this idea was percolating, we put our iPod on "shuffle" one day. Out of the past came a song by Kathy Trocolli: Go Light Your World. I dug around and found a book I'd purchased years ago that contained that song and wept as I played and sang these words:

Chorus:

Carry your candle, run to the darkness
Seek out the hopeless, confused and torn
Hold out your candle for all to see it
Take your candle, and go light your world
Take your candle, and go light your world
By Chris Rice

The Holy Spirit used this song to fan again the flame of my passion for souls in Greenville, the town where I never wanted to live. I've discovered He does that in many different ways. My dear cousin, Alma, who spent many hours with my grandfather, Mose Beachy, who died before I was born, said she credits him and his influence with her passion for souls. Now in her nineties, she still drives to a distant community to carry the light of Jesus to the lost. I'm moved by her passion and her faithfulness.

I believe the Holy Spirit birthed the idea of having a lighthouse on our property to renew my passion to be a light in our community. His heart is broken for those who are still in darkness and He wants to break our hearts with what breaks His.

Lord Jesus, we know that first of all, YOU
are the light of the world (John 8:12), but you also tell us that we
are the light of the world (Matthew 5:14). Break our hearts for
those who are still in darkness and make us passionate to allow
your light to shine through us. Amen.

ERICK'S DESIRE
November 07

Every time a letter arrives from our Compassion child in Tanzania, he begs us to come visit him and his family. Each time Donn and I shake our heads, seeing only the obstacles. Last month after Prayer for Greenville at Fresh Grounds, I found myself telling Nancy, a woman I knew to be a retired missionary, about this boy begging us to visit him in Tanzania.

She smiled and said, "You could go with me."

Surely my jaw dropped and I stared at her. "You go to Tanzania?"

"Every two years. I was a missionary there for a long time."

I couldn't believe my ears. If I had ever known Nancy had served in Tanzania, I had forgotten. She told me she was going to Tanzania in November but would be going again in two years if I couldn't be ready that soon. We talked about the cost and length of the plane flights, etc. What was God doing?

The next week at prayer for Downtown Ministries, I mentioned all this to those gathered, reiterating the possible challenges in-country even if I went to Tanzania with Nancy. Someone said, "Compassion used to arrange in-country visits for folks who want to visit their child. I don't know if they still do."

This was new information that raised my hopes again. A few days later, I spoke to a Compassion tour organizer who assured me this service *is* still available and clarified the options and a rough estimate of the costs. I hung up with the knowledge that while the trip would be expensive, a visit with Erick *was* possible. Since Compassion requires eight weeks notice, accompanying Nancy this year was definitely out, but the next trip might be a possibility.

I find it hard to believe that all of this is just a "coincidence," that the one person to whom I mentioned Erick's desire, goes to Tanzania every other year and would be delighted to have me accompany her. (She says I could stay with her at the seminary where she served.) Also, it's worth noting that someone at the FG prayer meeting knew that

Compassion used to provide this service, leading me to discover that they still do.

My heart has been so moved for months that this boy, whose family probably has next to nothing, longs to have us visit. In spite of our original reaction, I'm beginning to believe God placed that desire in his heart and wants to fulfill it.

Believe it or not, I am essentially a homebody—perfectly happy to never set foot outside the United States. But once again, I make of my body a living sacrifice for Jesus' sake and the sake of this child. If God wants me to go to Tanzania, He will continue to open every door and fulfill the desire of this young man's heart. Please pray with us for God's provision and health and strength for the journey.

(Author's Note August 11, 2022) Covid effectively shut down Compassion's in-country visits to Tanzania. My name is on a list to be called if in-country visits begin again.

UNEXAMINED LIVES
November 13

This summer our rose bush was covered with buds—Donn counted 50 or more. As the blooms opened, it was a beautiful sight. I was thrilled every time I looked at it. Then last week, I noticed little red spots on some of the blooms. I immediately consulted Google to find out what was causing the problem.

Different sites talked about a lethal disease that caused these spots on rose blooms, but all of them insisted the disease also affected the leaves. I was puzzled since I was sure the leaves of our rose were unaffected. However, when I checked them again to reassure myself, I discovered the upper leaves *were* fine. But hidden under the luscious blooms and glossy leaves, closer to the ground, were yellowed leaves and leaves with ugly black spots.

Donn and I had been so enthralled with all the buds and blossoms that we failed to notice the deadly disease that required closer examination to detect.

Our first foster son, age six or so, would sometimes say to us, "So, what's your point?" It always got a laugh, but it's a question I ask myself every week while writing blogs: "What's your point, Daisy?"

My point today is that we may become so dazzled by the "blooms" of our lives, the things that make us look good to others, whether it be ministry, service, or good deeds, that we find ourselves living "unexamined lives." Socrates is given credit for having said, *The unexamined life is not worth living.* I'm not sure exactly what he meant by that statement, but to me, the unexamined life is a life lived by a Christian who is so busy "doing" that no time is spent looking into the mirror of God's Word. No time is taken to listen and pray for God to examine his/her heart and life. Meanwhile the disease of sin gains ground, and we are completely unaware.

After reading I Corinthians 13, the author of The Cross and the Switchblade, David Wilkerson, said he looked into the mirror and saw a man who was "easily provoked." (V. 5 *(Love) is not easily provoked.)* The mirror of God's Word had shown him something about himself of which he was unaware, something he needed to allow God to change.

When I say we need to "look into the mirror of God's Word," I'm not talking about reading the Bible to prepare for preaching or teaching a message, Bible Study or Sunday School class. I heard about a pastor who went for counseling after having become involved in an affair. The counselor asked him, "How did it happen? How did you go from having a close walk with the Lord to having an affair?"

The fallen pastor said, "All my time in God's Word became preparation for ministry. I no longer had time to seek God for my own needs. My heart was empty and when the temptation came to fill it in other ways, I yielded."

James 1:23-24 NIV says, *Anyone who listens to the Word but does not do what it says is like someone who looks at his face in the mirror and after looking at himself, goes away immediately and forgets what he looks like.* So even when we spend time in God's Word for our own needs, we have the choice of whether or not we will act on what we read. But if we have the attitude of King David in Psalms 139:23-24 (see below), the Holy Spirit will be faithful to point out the disease of sin before it causes devastation. (KJV says "wicked way," but I like this translation better since we are easily convinced that wicked does not apply to us.)

Search me, God, and know my heart;
test me and know my anxious thoughts.
See if there is any offensive way in me,
and lead me in the way everlasting
(Psalm 139:23-24).

MY SISTER SANDRA
December 11

"...the most beautiful voice I ever heard spoke my name. 'Sandra, take the bullets out of the gun.'"

The people around our dining room table were spellbound listening to the testimony of Sandra Wright, the song evangelist at our church's mission conference in the early ninties. My "writer's ears" pricked up, sensing a story worth writing.

This encounter around our table led to *Touched by Grace,* an article published in Guideposts in August, 1995, (for which I was Sandra's "ghost writer") and a lifelong friendship with my sister, Sandra.

Since she lived in Meadville and I lived in Sandy Lake, it took intentional planning for our friendship to flourish, but it was so worth it. Our birthdays were just five days apart, so we often planned a get-together in June, and usually saw each other more frequently than that. If I was going to Meadville or Erie, I often called or just stopped by to visit. Sometimes we made plans for her to come to Sandy Lake.

I also visited Sandra in the hospital at various times when health issues took her there. I don't remember why Sandra was in the hospital on this occasion or what we were discussing, but I remember quoting this phrase from "When I Survey the Wondrous Cross:" *Love so amazing so divine, demands my soul, my life, my all.* Sandra got her *Oh, this blesses me so much* look and said, "Say that again, Sister Daisy." She closed her eyes and soaked up the truth of songwriter, Isaac Watts' words. It was the desire of her heart to serve her Savior in a way that demanded her soul, her life, her all.

Our friendship was a two-way street. Sometimes I picked her up when she was down, at other times she did the same for me. When I was struggling during our ministry in Japan, Sandra asked me succinctly, "Have you found your 'God-place' over there yet?" (She knew that Presque Isle in Erie was my God-place in the U.S.) When I said, "No," she answered, "You'd better be finding it!" I did find it at the Shinjuku Goen (Park) and God met me there.

On November 20, 2019, while I was having my quiet time, I received what would be my last communication from Sandra. She began as she often did, "Hello, my flower friend. I'm texting to ask for prayer and to let you know I'm in the hospital for heart surgery." (Followed, of course, by a purple heart—Sandra loved purple and hearts.)

I'm so thankful I responded immediately to learn more about her condition and then to pray with her online. I prayed for healing, of course, not knowing that the Lord would choose to heal her completely by taking her to heaven a few days later.

While I have no doubt that God was not surprised by any of this, I was unprepared to lose the earthly presence of my friend. The past five years or so, my attempts to get together had often failed and too much time had passed since I'd seen her, although we kept in touch through Facebook. But I'm so thankful Sandra reached out to me one more time before her final journey. Our last exchange on Messenger has become so precious to me.

She ended our conversation by saying, "Thank you my dear sister." (And of course, another purple heart.) Thank you, my dear Sister Sandra, for the joy and privilege of being your friend. My life has been richer and more blessed because of our friendship. Save a place for me!

Father, thank you for connecting us
with people who enrich our lives and share the joy
of being brothers and sisters in Christ.
Give Sister Sandra our love as she enjoys the
pleasure of your presence in a greater way than every before. Amen.

... in your presence is fullness of joy (Psalm 16:11).

OTHER BOOKS BY
DAISY BEILER TOWNSEND

HOMESPUN FAITH
(Reflections on the Seasons of Life)

SARAH'S LEGACY
SARAH'S LEGACY SHARED
SARAH'S LEGACY TESTED
SARAH'S LEGACY LIVED